MW01516744

Praise for *Fixing Fractures,* Do

"Doug Bouey's 'Fixing Fractures' is the practical, 'How To' field guide and roadmap to eliminating the destructive conflict that impedes our progress, and ultimately derails our dreams of a happy and productive life."

Scott Morris,
Founder and Former CEO – Results.com

"The pandemic has sharply brought awareness to me that there are two types of people when it comes to personal relationships. There are those you realize aren't really that important to you and then there are those who you really want to spend time with.

Doug's book reminds me there are those in the second group we have lost that connection to. Maybe it was broken awhile back and we're not sure how to fix it. The journey he takes us on may be a winding road, but it's easy to follow; helping to repair those vital lost relationships that many people have given up on."

Grant Ainsley,
Media and Communication Trainer

"I love Fixing Fractures. This book contains the truth of relationships in a simple way. If you want a short cut, this isn't for you. Your wit is unique.

I'm buying your book for my managers."

Derek Bullen,
President, Si Systems Ltd.

"In my 22 years as Vistage Chair, I have facilitated conversations that are so difficult and with so much at stake. I wish I had Fixing Fractures as a conversation guide while coaching CEOs... when every word choice, every gesture, intentionality, and the whole relationship mattered. Follow this guide – every step – the next time you want to repair a relationship. Every leader should read it at least once and keep it handy. It will work!"

Nora Paller,
Vistage Master Chair

"This book provides us all with a structured methodology to help us navigate our way through really uncomfortable conflict situations. Following an approach like this, gives us confidence in achieving the best possible outcome to what feels like an impossible situation. For people who don't feel confident enough to embark on this themselves, it is an excellent tool that an experienced coach or mediator can provide help with. In any case, it is always good to know what steps are required to get things back on track and the responsibilities you have along the way. I also highly recommend listening to the audio version of "Fixing Fractures" where Doug reads the book himself."

Joyce Hookings

"If you coach and mentor CEOs, Presidents, and other business leaders, I guarantee that "Fixing Fractures" will become an indispensable resource for you.

This little guidebook will help you deal with very contentious interpersonal situations; I know you will find it extremely helpful."

Peter Buchanan,
Preeminent Canadian TEC/ Vistage
Chair and Development Head

"Thoroughly enjoyed reading your new book Fixing Fractures. I love your use of the Kintsugi metaphor. Fits like a hand in a glove.

Your 8-step process for restoring trust is truly powerful. To paraphrase your words: Perseverance through extravagant patience, care, and rising above difficulty and obstacles works. Embracing damage can allow a fractured relationship to heal, grow anew, and become solid once again. Gold filled cracks, and all.

Willie Rosoff,
Master Vistage Chair

FIXING FRACTURES

Restoring shattered relationships in business and in life

Douglas R. Bouey
realized with Lois Wozney

With foreword by Susan Scott

Scenarios in this book are fictitious.
Any similarity to actual persons, living
or dead, is coincidental.
Every effort has been made to contact
all copyright holders.

Copyright © 2021 Douglas Robert Bouey
Cover and interior artwork copyright
© 2021 Alejandro Anaya
All rights reserved. No part of this book may be
reproduced or used in any manner without the
prior written permission of the copyright owner,
except for the use of brief quotations in a book review.
To request permission, contact the author
at Douglas@DougBouey.com

Book	ISBN #978-1-7779721-0-3
Electronic Book	ISBN #978-1-7779721-1-0
Hardcover Book	ISBN #978-1-7779721-2-7
Audio Book	ISBN #978-1-7779721-3-4

First paperback edition January 2022

Edited by	Lois Wozney
Artwork by	Alejandro Anaya
Layout by	Jana Rade

Foreword

I was incredibly honored when Doug invited me to write the foreword to this wonderful book. And it IS wonderful. There is so much pain from fractured relationships, when trust is lacking. When we've lost a relationship that was important and valuable, the aftermath is ongoing and deadly. Thoughts about the loss distracts us, dominates our thoughts, hurts, even makes us sick, literally. If we pretend it's in the past and we can just move on without a backward glance, our failure to do our best to regain the relationship feels like an integrity outage. And this is true for all those around us… within our companies, our families. The "wound" is real and is in the way.

Those familiar with my work know that I believe our most valuable currency isn't money, charisma, fluency in 3-letter acronyms, or pedigree. Our most valuable currency is relationship – emotional capital – which we gain or lose, one conversation at a time. In fact, the conversation *is* the relationship. In *Fixing Fractures*, Doug provides a clear and compelling roadmap for the needed conversation, not only to restore a relationship that fell off the cliff, but to greatly enrich it, improve it, deepen it.

This book is for anyone – that would be you and me – who wants to resolve a difficult, daunting, persistent and occasionally volatile issue with someone important to their success and happiness.

And may I add that I love the way Doug writes. This is not a dry book with a professorial tone. It is human, real and often humorous. You'll learn about "sucker's tennis", be warned about a "flight into health" and enjoy such wisdom as: **"We don't teach this to provide you with tools for more enlightened blaming!**

Heaping handfuls of gratitude for this book, Doug!

Susan Scott
June 2021

FierceInc.com
Facebook: Susan Scott Fierce

Fierce Conversations – Achieving Success at Work & in Life, One Conversation at a Time

Fierce Leaderships – A Bold Alternative to the Worst "Best" Practices in Business Today

Fierce Love – Creating a Love That Lasts, One Conversation at a Time (January 2022)

"In nature, the evolution of growth and life cannot continue without differences and opposition. Yet the root cause of most failures in relationships and organizations is our inability to relate to these natural forces in a positive and effective way.

We relate to:
change as a threat
differences as a problem
opposition as an attack

We relate poorly to each other because we relate poorly to the processes of nature."

— John Konstanturos

An invitation

Friends: we come together for a solemn and noble purpose – to liberate good people from prison.

It's a prison two people entered after something happened. They had been parties in an important relationship – one that was very meaningful to both. But there was a misfire, and their formerly free and easy association broke down. Walls came up. Positive interactions were either cut off or became hard labor. There seemed to be no chance for it to change. It was bad and set to stay that way.

Relationships between humans that work well are key to constructive living. When they go sideways, they get messy, crabbed, fraught with angry grudges, feuds, impasses, resentment, regret, guilt… Most of us have experienced the sudden chill of a damaged bond with someone who matters. Have you? Few of us have learned how to fully restore a fractured relationship to one that's whole and vibrant.

Do you find yourself no longer able to interact easily with a certain colleague, relative, friend? Is there a business player with whom you shared a mission but who has broken with you? Has someone you were once close to become standoffish or distant? If so, you're only human. And if you mourn that loss and want to do something about it, you've arrived at the right place.

This book is a guide to help you set a relationship fracture right. It promises resolution. It aims your sights beyond mere settlement and helps you shoot for the moon:

- A contentious dilemma, thoroughly disarmed
- A conclusion to the issue, without loose ends left to fester
- A future where the matter never comes up again

There is nothing exactly like it.

Kintsugi – the metaphor on the cover

Kintsugi – only the Japanese could conceive an art form centered on breakage and repair of something precious. Kintsugi involves dropping a porcelain container as a starting point. And Kintsugi is an entirely apt analogy for what this book enables you to do… take a vessel of great value that seems irrevocably, hopelessly broken and put it back together, in a form more noble and admirable than it was prior to breaking.

How is it done? The Japanese traditional art encompasses gathering the pieces, then painstakingly refitting, and gluing them together with using a gold mortar. Perseverance is the byword. Through extravagant patience, care, and rising above difficulty and obstacles, the damage is made whole.

For this book, a ceramic bucket can represent the trust, warmth, and interdependence between two parties. This 'trust bucket' has been shattered. Using the Resolution Protocol, it is reassembled. Truth is, the wonder of that bucket becomes much more evident with the renaissance that began the moment it shattered. An exquisite solvent for sadness will be applied. The gold of dedication will become the glue of restoration.

This book is about transformation. In undertaking the discipline you will discover here, you accept and elevate what we all must suffer by our presence in the world. You will lift yourself above woundedness and see a relationship differently – in a way that's much more connected to what matters.

The outcome is a creation to joyfully behold, and newly cherish. A relationship broken, made whole and much better, more resilient and magnificent than it ever was before.

Contents

Foreword 7

An invitation. 11

Contents 15

A handbook 17

The travelers and the journey 19

When is it time? 27

Get organized for the trip 31

The road you travel; one incident 37

Set the date; start the car 43

Step 1 – Buckle in; my roles and relationship to you . . 53

Step 2 – The facts; your bumpy road 59

Rest stop! A guidance system for a turbulent ride. . . . 69

Step 3 – The driver; emotions and identity 85

Step 4 – Over the bridge; take radical ownership 97

Pit stop! Amp up awareness; be ready to really listen . 109

Step 5 – The view from there. 125

Step 6 – Recenter on your destination; recalculating... 145

Step 7 – Negotiation; onward with your adventure . . 157

Step 8 – Arrive in style; confirmation
and commitment 175

Epilogue 183

Afterword and recap 185

Appendices 189
     Appendix A – It won't work when.... 191
     Appendix B – Recommended reading. 197

Fixing Fractures Toolkit. 199
     The Resolution Protocol on a Page 201
     The Resolution Guidance System on a Page . . 203
     The Preparation Worksheet 205

Fixing Fractures – the fast lane 209

Acknowledgements 217

Profiles. 219

A handbook

This is a handbook – a set of instructions for how to solve specific problems between people. You picked it up because you are curious and perhaps eager to learn how to fix a messy situation with an important person.

As a handbook, this slim volume includes just enough background for you to understand the *what* and *why* of getting to the bottom of a gnarly situation. But mainly it is written so you can also get right to the *how* and *when*. It is a practical guide and a ready reference for anyone to use.

This is an approach to settling serious, daunting problems between people. Can it work in all situations? Look to the Appendix where I describe a few situations where it shouldn't be attempted. Nevertheless, it's suited to bringing *most* fragmented situations to closure.

It consists of four central components, working together:

- **The Relationship Mindset** – an orientation to human interaction that frames and nurtures interpersonal connections
- **The Resolution Protocol** – an eight-step structured process to guide an intense resolution talk
- **The Pre-Work** – indispensable advance preparation
- **The Flow** – a way to chair and steer the conversation

How to use this book

Step by step, I guide you through the phases of resolution. Along the way you pick up the tools to apply to your own situation. Each chapter:

- Explains a component of the Resolution Protocol or expands on an aspect of the Relationship Mindset
- Outlines the preparation required
- Discusses some practical realities
- Illuminates useful concepts with clarifying stories
- Builds your resolution skills and confidence

A summary of key points in all the chapters is provided in the Appendix for ready reference later.

After this has landed with you, consider reading Susan Scott's *Fierce Conversations*. She and I are much aligned on the purpose of resolution conversations – to interrogate reality, provoke learning, tackle tough challenges, enrich relationships.

Are you willing to change your perspective to achieve a result you greatly desire? To make things right with a person you really care about?

The travelers and the journey

Fact: a relationship is fractured and needs to mend.

Fact: the Resolution Protocol sorts out the messy situation so that the parties prosper together once again, and the cause of the break never recurs.

This book asks you to take a journey – a set of constructive steps along a defined path where you first examine the break, then re-set and secure it so it can heal properly. Your time is spent on the road to your destination, not waiting for a miracle in hospital!

As with any venture into uncharted territory, you need courage to stay the course and face the issues, your fellow traveler, and yourself.

We designate two characters on this resolution passage.

The Initiator

This is you – the person devoting time to learning the Resolution Protocol and who is courageous enough to initiate and conduct a serious talk regarding a rift with...

The Very Important Person (VIP)

This is your counterpart, the other person on the path with you. I call them the VIP because you care about them and their worth so much that you are willing to traverse deep valleys to restore your once-close tie with them. By that measure, naturally they are a VIP. They remain so despite how cross you have been about what happened between you, or how often you have been sorely tempted to write them off.

It all starts with you

If you want to use this approach to fix a relationship in your life that's gone askew, you must first know what the Resolution Protocol requires of you. You can certainly do this, but your eyes must be open to the effort required to rectify the breakdown.

It's not enough to go only partway along the path, or just dip your toe in the process. To achieve resolution, you must take on the discipline, commit yourself to the entirety and stay the course – from raising the issue through to celebrating its conclusion.

The Resolution Protocol is a proven way to sort out such situations so that they never recur – that's the true test of resolution. The relationship fracture is healed.

You too can attain that high bar by following the steps and guidance in this book. It won't be an argument about who's right. It will be an intense discussion to break down the prison walls, get to the roots of what went wrong, and do what it takes to make it right.

What do you need most? Undaunted courage. Enough to not only face the issue, and your other party, but most importantly, to face yourself.

If you're looking for a quick way to deliver an ultimate defeat, to finish off another person with a masterful stroke, this isn't the book for you.

Situations that demand such exemplary drive to confront are onerous, complex, and gritty messes, like the story of David and Leonora that is woven through this handbook. As with them, if the pain of your fracture is acute, and the relationship important enough, you will rise to the challenge of this journey.

Congratulations

You chose this book because despite the risks and your fears, you have decided to put matters right. You realize that if you don't act to heal this break, you'll regret it for the rest of your life. You won't go unprepared on this trip. With this book as your guide, you'll feel ready and able to take on this deeply important conversation.

The Resolution Protocol is simple but robust. It is designed for tough situations. **It works** because you put your whole heart and mind into it. You agree to head into unfamiliar territory and expose your vulnerability along the way. Much depends on your ability to be authentic, to deliver the messages of this process and maximize the potential for change.

With all that, walking through a tough situation and taking it over the finish line to resolution is one of the most **satisfying** things you will ever do in life. It's profound. These conversations often become etched in the memories of the parties, and are turning points in their lives.

Let me introduce you to David and Leonora, executives of Dugmore Foods. You'll get to know their story as we follow along their resolution journey, and see the process as it unfolds. While this story is focused on a business scenario, use of the Protocol isn't restricted to that domain. It applies between relatives, friends, neighbors, spouses…wherever relationships that matter arise.

The moment it came to a head

On this day, David is leading an Operations Forum meeting, where a group of four are readying for a production run of Almond Sky – one of Dugmore Foods' prime offerings. They are going through the critical readiness checklist for a run set to proceed later that day. When they review supply quantities, Leonora – the logistics lead – offhandedly mentions, "We might be short on flour." Sarah rolls her eyes. Fernando looks askance. The atmosphere quickly gets heavy in that second-floor boardroom.

David's guts turn to water. This run is for is their lead product and backorders are accelerating! Leonora's unconcerned remark just lays there, as if someone has thrown a carcass on the table.

David's thoughts knot up, and he thinks to himself…

"Here we go again! Am I going to have to fire this hotshot…?

Wait a minute. I can't! She's my peer. And she's family.

What's going to come down on me when I have to tell the President about this…? I can't just say nothing! Leonora's so good most of the time, but this last-minute rabbit-out-of-a-hat stuff makes me crazy! I can't stand it…!"

confused process. It increased delivery reliability, and the firm's fortunes rose. The VP designation followed. His reputation and career success were based on that bankable dependability...

When is it time?

The Resolution Protocol is designed specifically for people in truly tough binds. It's too intensive a process to use for an everyday slight disagreement, a minor contretemps, or even a fair-sized quarrel. How do you know you need to have one of these resolution talks? When should you bring out the heavy artillery... this intentional approach?

*"Because the heart is
bigger than trouble*

And the heart is bigger than doubt

*The heart some times needs a
little help to figure that out."*

– CONNIE KALDOR
"WOOD RIVER"

Everything that occurs in a relationship fills or draws down on your metaphorical *bucket of trust*. You come to expect an individual to react a certain way, and count on an unstated belief – right or wrong – that you will interact with each other in a reliable, regular style. You extend implicit trust and hope it will be honoured.

A serious situation doesn't usually arise overnight. You sail along having comfortable exchanges that fill up that bucket. But you start to get hints that something is not right. And then one day, a truly problematic episode occurs. Your trust bucket fractures catastrophically and drains dry. **You feel betrayed.**

When trust is badly compromised, you might notice:

- The precipitating situation just wouldn't go away. It pops up and is on your mind whenever you're reminded of that person or situation.
- You find yourself reprocessing the lead-up to the break. Suggestions that it was coming had been manifesting for some time. You recognize

just how off-track your relationship had become before trust broke.

- Now it swirls within you. You dwell on what happened, what was said and done. You ruminate over what could or should have occurred, or how you might have avoided such a hard landing with this person.
- You rationalize and justify your own stance, persuading yourself that you were right and the other person was wrong.
- You think of rejoinders or clever retorts you might have made. If you had come up with the right one at the critical moment, you might have headed off this mess. But it's too late.
- Damage has been accumulating since the break. That assessment crystallizes a need in you to take a definitive step and intervene, before things go from bad to worse. Not just between the two of you, but for others as well – in the business, among friends or family. Many are adversely affected, treading carefully around the matter. Meanwhile, performance is dropping, needed collaboration becomes impossible, events where you both are present are strained and forced, and attention is diverted from the real purpose. A whole bunch of folks are dancing around your dysfunction.
- The realization hits. *This is worse than I thought. I'd better do something.*

Recognize yourself in these descriptions? It's time to study the Resolution Protocol and get to work preparing for a very consequential conversation.

Seize the opportunity, initiate a resolution talk, and be glad of it for years to come. Or turn away, ignore those pesky barbs, and resign yourself to spiralling, distancing negativity. It's up to you.

Get organized for the trip

Relying on instinct alone won't get you where you want to go. Gear up with the right stuff for the road – the road to repair.

Four key components help you capitalize on your courage and face into the breach. Avoid old, failed tactics, and head direct to your destination… nothing less than a restored and optimal relationship with your VIP.

Component 1 – The Resolution Protocol

This is the simple, clean recipe to follow so the Initiator (you) can maximize the potential for positive correction and change. The wisdom of the Protocol will grow on you, particularly its stepwise progression of topics.

STEP 1	Describe **your role and relationship** to the other person.
STEP 2	Outline the **facts of a single incident** that led to the relationship break.
STEP 3	Express ***your* emotional reaction** to the situation and its impact on your identity.
STEP 4	**Declare your part** in creating or continuing the situation.
STEP 5	**Listen to *their* version** of what happened, and *their* emotional reaction.
STEP 6	Describe **your expectations** of what is required to set matters right.
STEP 7	**Negotiate** a path forward to rectify the situation.
STEP 8	**Clarify** your new agreement, and **affirm** your restored **common purpose.**

With this list in hand, you *could* just start in on these steps, and plunge into a confrontational chat. But why not go easy on yourself? Spend some time learning the remaining three components of the framework: the Relationship Mindset, the Pre-Work, and the Flow.

Component 2 – The Relationship Mindset

The Protocol is your *program*, but it won't run right without its *operating system* – the Relationship Mindset. Grounded in heightened awareness, the Mindset is the strong foundation that balances and infuses the Protocol steps with grace and compassion. Without it, the Resolution Protocol is just a recipe. With it, the Protocol is animated – and the combination is unstoppable.

The Mindset is made up of attitudes and viewpoints that weave together to strengthen empathy and understanding. I'll explore each of these Mindset topics:

- The nature of difference – how to regard conflict
- Fractured trust – the source of exploded expectations
- The truth – always unfolding
- The beach ball – we see the situation differently
- Boundaries – the inner sense of trespass
- 100% → 0% – the only productive counter to the blame game
- The Resolution Guidance System – visualize your intuition to steer an unpredictable conversation

Component 3 – The Pre-Work

Would you go unprepared into a business meeting where the topic is of critical impact? Would you go cold into a delicate interview seeking financing from your banker? Would you waltz into a must-win sales presentation and just wing it?

I suspect you would prepare ahead of time: do some research, be ready to state clearly why you're there, talk about past dealings, express your goals, actively explore the other's perspective, and generate ideas for next steps.

A successful resolution conversation is based on the Initiator's written preparation. To help you get ready for this sensitive talk, a Preparation Worksheet form is available in the Appendix for you to fill out ahead of time. It is also available at *DougBouey.com/ffdownloads*.

You might have one beside you now, and get your talk ready as you go through this handbook...

Using the Worksheet, you go step-by-step through your situation, organize your thoughts, and ready the words you need. As a bonus, this effort calms your nerves.

Component 4 – The Flow

Following the steps of the Protocol, the conversation goes back and forth in an orderly way:

Steps 1-4	The Initiator speaks, with few interruptions
Step 5	The VIP responds
Step 6	The Initiator leads
Steps 7-8	The Initiator and VIP collaborate jointly

As Initiator, you take strong leadership, particularly for Steps 1 through 4. This means you will be acting the way a meeting Chairperson would. You may need to ask your VIP to hold off commenting until you finish a section. This may feel unfamiliar and uncomfortable to you.

Other times you hand the floor to your VIP, yet still manage the Flow from the back seat. Overall, you will gently guide the conversation through the Protocol structure.

All together now...

These components – the Resolution Protocol, the Relationship Mindset, the Pre-Work, and the Flow – are the framework for a process that *works*. **They all go together, and maximize the impact of what is said in the resolution conversation.**

- The Resolution Protocol – the roadmap to take you to your destination
- The Relationship Mindset – the rules of the road for safe driving
- The Pre-Work – the fuel you need for the trip
- The Flow – who drives, and when

When these four pieces knit together, you will see two competent people in full possession of themselves who can sit down together to address a very difficult subject, and take it right through to conclusion. They can venture into a highly charged discussion and persist, remaining grounded and self-controlled, from beginning to end.

Eager to get going? Before you launch, stay with me awhile. You want to be fully briefed and at your best for this talk.

So, what *do* you talk about? In the next chapter I'll help you focus down on one incident; the key that gets you started.

The road you travel; one incident

This chapter is about choosing a focus. It's your first task when you sit down to complete your Preparation Worksheet. **Zero in** on just one representative incident and make it the avenue by which you safely enter the resolution zone with your VIP.

Which one? Perhaps there are several candidates. You may want to go over the entire course of conduct between the two of you, looking for a situation where the whole dysfunctional dynamic crystallized. But don't work too hard at making the perfect choice. It should be recent – one that the VIP is likely to recall. If one circumstance in particular seems supercharged, gets your hackles up, and is one you'd rather avoid mentioning, that's probably it.

One. That's all. The truth is, any one would suffice because each situation illustrates and has contributed to what's off between you.

Without this singular focus, as soon as you're face to face you will be tempted to set the other person straight, explaining all the reasons why their current and past actions cause you distress.

Imagine for a moment that someone sat you down to point out all your errors in action or judgement, incident after incident, highlighting your faults. Of course, you'd go right into self-defence mode, probably be emotionally ravaged, and maybe just shut down completely. Garbage-pail fighting – piling everything on – makes the receiver a target. It puts them in the goal net while you take hundreds of shots at them. Their only recourse is self-protection.

You don't want to flatten your VIP! It doesn't work. You more than value and respect them, you care about them. This is where you begin to separate from the way you've been thinking about this situation so far. That's the Relationship Mindset taking hold.

You want to encourage and enable their ability to:

- join in a constructive dialogue,
- meet you squarely,
- stay with you throughout the Protocol, and
- deal with the problem.

This is why you are meeting in the first place. You already decided that to pillory your VIP, or cut them out of your life is no solution. Beneath the turmoil of your difficult situation, you hope and believe in the possibility of constructive restoration of your relationship. Your conscience is driving you to give that possibility a chance.

You are getting on board with a Relationship Mindset. It equips and compels you to engage in and emerge from this important talk not only whole, but vastly improved. Both of you!

If you just want to deliver summary justice to a dimwit who deserves it, put this book down. You don't need to dress up your intent. Just close this book and go ahead. Blast away. Reading on will not give you a silver bullet.

Also, don't send this book to someone as a hint that they should get their act together. They won't realize what you're suggesting, and will probably just be more offended.

So, rather than overwhelm your VIP, step back from the belief that you must *win*, and accept that change is your metric of success. It's what you seek to do… ensure that both of you are competently able to have a conversation focused on what can change, alter, or fix the dynamic.

Commit to avoid talking about everything, and select an incident. Don't fret about it. Just pick one, write it down at the top of your Preparation Worksheet, and get to work on your resolution journey.

Being Leonora

Bearing visible tattoos on both bare arms and a shock of pink hair, Leonora is not your typical logistics expert. She became one via an unconventional route.

Her parents had sent her off to college, hoping to give her obvious intelligence some running room. However, Leonora went in a completely unanticipated direction. She fed her rebel streak and moved to Venice Beach to be close to the ocean. But the beach was expensive and even with two roommates, she soon ran out of cash to support her free life style. Since her parents had 'released her to industry', and having no other recourse, she joined LogoStar as a driver.

Her job was to pick up materials the company needed on short notice; LogoStar was proud of its just-in-time approach to manufacturing. She quickly solved most of the short-notice issues that had made the firm need a driver in the first place. And, despite her unusual appearance, the brass at LogoStar saw her potential. She began to rise swiftly in the ranks.

One night at a party in Huntington, she met Raymond, another free spirit. He mirrored her appetite for the unusual, and was a bit of a black sheep in a family whose patriarch just happened to run a large food processing company.

They became entangled and pretty soon, against her history, started making plans.

It was after their civil wedding ceremony out on the Santa Monica Pier that Ray's father, comfortable in his traditional grey suit despite the wilder attire of most guests, sidled up to the resplendent bride in her backless crimson gown,

"I'd like to talk to you when you're back from the honeymoon…"

With that special induction and ready for a change, Leonora looked into Dugmore Foods, LogoStar's larger competitor. After her job interview, Dugmore's Chief Financial Officer observed, "She has sass, I'll give her that!"

Lenora became an excellent young logistics specialist in Dugmore's Operations division. She loved the work and retained her edge. She and Ray frequented the beach clubs and followed the local music scene. Still in their twenties, they were feeling their oats, together.

Leonora was a powerhouse at work, and knew it. Dugmore was a much larger enterprise and had a mandate to supply products to the entire western half of the continent. She had many more balls to juggle. After three years on the job, she seemed to handle it well.

She became Dugmore's upstart VP of Logistics and part of the Operations Forum because of her drive and ability to respond to changing situations. Lately though, she had almost shorted a few exceptionally critical ingredients for Dugmore's top products. Leonora just dismissed how close the company had come to stocking-out, and proudly told people how 'her side' (as she termed her team) had pulled off some last-minute saves. In their huddles, the team crowed about their just-in-time philosophy and exploits. They mocked the staid production types, who always needed everything battened down way before it was needed. Leonora didn't discourage them.

As Operations VP, David dreaded the idea of supply shortages happening again and having a real show-stopper on his hands.

Except for her nonchalance about supply levels, Leonora had tons of smarts and potential. But her tendency to let inventories get a little too thin disturbed David, and eroded his confidence in her. He'd been pretty distraught that first time… down to just a half-ton of supply for one of the cookie lines, and only one day away from shut-down! Leonora had been able to secure the needed materials in time, and even joked about David's apprehension. But then it happened a second and third time.

And now he had a memo from his father-in-law (the CEO) in his inbox: *"I'm hearing of disagreements between Logistics and Production. The cooperation of these groups is absolutely crucial to our growth. I don't like this undertone. You guys better get your act together…"*

He got out a Preparation Worksheet and started writing…

When do you approach your VIP? How do you set up, then start in on the conversation? That's coming up next.

Set the date; start the car

It's time to head out on your trip. In sequence:

- Read this book all the way through first!
- Then, turn to your own troubling situation, select an incident, and fill out a Preparation Worksheet, following along with the book.

- Next, set up a meeting time and place to talk with your VIP.
- And initiate the conversation.

Written preparation

In a face-to-face discussion of this consequence, you must anticipate that both the direction of the talk and your memory will be impaired by fierce emotion.

I've taught and practised this approach for thirty years. Whenever I need to have an important conversation, I still write out my preparation in full. I never take chances with such potentially explosive material.

A Preparation Worksheet template is available in the Appendix or at *DougBouey.com/ffdownloads.*

With the Worksheet for reference **in your hand**, you will be better able to stay on track as you move through the Protocol steps:

STEP 1	Describe **your role and relationship** to the other person.
STEP 2	Outline the **facts of a single incident** that led to the relationship break.
STEP 3	Express **_your_ emotional reaction** to the situation and its impact on your identity.
STEP 4	**Declare your part** in creating or continuing the situation.
STEP 5	**Listen to _their_ version** of what happened, and _their_ emotional reaction.
STEP 6	Describe **your expectations** of what is required to set matters right.
STEP 7	**Negotiate** a path forward to rectify the situation.
STEP 8	**Clarify** your new agreement, and **affirm** your restored **common purpose.**

Writing assignments

Preparatory writing is required for Steps 1, 2, 3, 4 and 6. The Protocol and this handbook will sustain you, as you dry-run each of these steps on paper. No advance writing is required for Steps 5, 7 and 8, beyond a couple of reminders or prompts on your Worksheet.

- *For Step 1* – Describe the type and scope of the **roles** you occupy in relation to your VIP – the ways you connect with them. There are often several, and they may overlap.
- *For Step 2* – Outline **what happened** – what the hard evidence says actually took place, captured in a chronological timeline.
- *For Step 3* – Express the **feelings** you encountered as this charged timeline unfolded. Name your specific emotions – variations of mad / sad / glad / scared.
- *For Step 4* – Declare **your part** in creating or continuing the situation. Set aside your ego and be completely truthful.
- *For Step 6* – Describe how you want **things to be different** when your relationship is back on track. What are your new expectations?

 Find some undisturbed time to write; it's quite a soul-searching expedition. Most people are surprised by how much they need to get down, once they think about the situation anew.

So now, with your Preparation Worksheet in front of you, put distractions aside and devote some uninterrupted time to preparation. You will be glad of every second spent on it.

Crisp, clean, clear

In conventional conversation, you may just blurt out everything you feel needs to be said. Preparatory writing helps you be selective, to streamline your thoughts, and take care with your words. You can take a second (or third!) look at what you propose to say, and guard against including any bias, manipulation, or attempts to gain advantage.

Refine your thoughts on paper so you can get to the point quickly and accurately, and your counterpart knows exactly what you mean. Write to gain confidence in what you will (and won't) say in the moment. With a little care and revision, you can be just like Switzerland – crisp, clean, clear. And neutral!

In the chapters ahead, you'll get more information about the purpose and detail of each writing task. I urge you to take time to do this well; push for substance. Go below the surface rather than simply answering the Worksheet questions.

The appointment

Once your Preparation Worksheet is completed and in hand, you are ready to start the car, and approach your VIP to begin the journey.

I recognize that raising the issue triggers the most apprehension of the entire process. Here's how to do it:

- First find a neutral location where you and your counterpart can speak directly and confidentially, without interruption.
- Then, request a meeting. Say what it's about. It's best to be quick and to the point.

Here are some examples to help you craft your own words that invite your VIP to join you on the resolution trail:

I'd like to speak to you about [the incident]. Can we meet at...

This issue is really troubling me and getting in the way of us being effective together. I want to address it properly with you. Would you meet me privately at...

I'd like to talk to you about the proposal you raised in the last budget committee meeting. Can you please set aside an hour in Meeting Room B at 4:00 pm this afternoon?

That's it, no more. You only need to give them a sense of what's up. Chances are good they'll clue in to the issue as soon as you request the meeting – it's probably as sensitive to them as it is to you. Avoid the urge to reveal the whole enchilada then and there. Likewise, ask them to hold their horses until then, so you can both have a full and considered talk.

What if...

Your big deal may be a minor thing to them. They may have suppressed the memory of it and say something dismissive like, "That's all done now; I'm over it."

They may not want to talk at all. They may seem closed off, disinterested, their heart not in it.

They might meet your suggestion with an angry, sharp retort. Some people are excellent defenders of their position and respond vigorously. It's evidence of bruising and sensitivity, and confirms that you're on the nerve.

Such responses illustrate the sometimes-unpredictable process of raising and dealing with issues. You may be seriously uneasy about even broaching an issue because you expect just such indifferent, unenthusiastic, or angry responses.

Your initial reaction should be to bend, like bamboo in a windstorm. Then lean back into your purpose for having this talk, and convey your desire to have an opportunity to give the issues the attention they properly deserve. It's the Relationship Mindset in action. Your empathy and compassion counteract their resistance. Rather than meeting their force with a counterforce, your best tack is to simply acknowledge their apparent indifference or sensitivity.

It's now that you need to trust your native intelligence and ability to respond constructively. No instruction book can provide recipes for every situation. Your improvisation in the moment will be fine, even if it seems clumsy to you right then.

I assure you that your caring intentions, and your serious purpose in resurrecting this thorny topic will come to your aid… will help both of you, really. The intent to adopt this structured process, and the effort you put into a well-completed Worksheet will prove their value in this moment.

Don't be surprised if you are rebuffed at first. And that your VIP comes back to you later, expressing greater willingness to engage.

In my experience, it's the initial broaching of the topic that Initiators fear the most, as they contemplate dealing with the fracture. I've taken a deeper dive in this chapter so you can be better prepared to deal with the response to your meeting invitation. Getting past this hurdle will hearten you, and give you confidence that you're on the right path.

I have occasionally been surprised that a VIP just can't hold back. They may want to get right into it. This isn't a great idea; it's likely to fire some old circuits and recycle the original wound. Still, you must anticipate the possibility.

Have your Preparation Worksheet with you, and be set to assume leadership and direction of the conversation in that moment – as soon as you can both get to a suitable location where you won't be overheard or interrupted.

In the following chapters I'll provide detailed guidance for each topic you'll prepare. I'll also help you understand what to expect as your own conversation unfolds in real life.

You're doing the good work. You have found focus and clarified a single difficult incident and are mobilized. Time to get onto the roadway and enroute to your destination.

Step 1

Buckle in; my roles and relationship to you

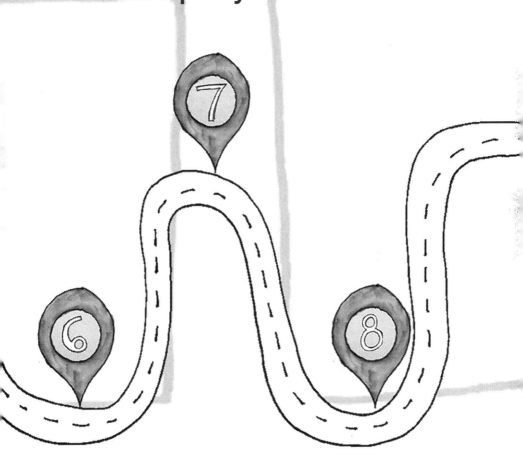

The Resolution Protocol

STEP 1   **Describe your role and relationship to the other person.**

STEP 2   Outline the facts of a single incident that led to the relationship break.

STEP 3   Express your emotional reaction to the situation and its impact on your identity.

STEP 4   Declare your part in creating or continuing the situation.

STEP 5   Listen to *their* version of what happened, and *their* emotional reaction.

STEP 6   Describe your expectations of what is required to set matters right.

STEP 7   Negotiate a path forward to rectify the situation.

STEP 8   Clarify your new agreement, and affirm your restored common purpose.

You've identified the single incident and have a view into the initial components of this work.

Your next writing assignment on the Preparation Worksheet is to list the ways you and your VIP interact. It's a simple and rich exercise of dual significance – it confirms your formerly shared connections, and sets out a basis for the reinvigorated relationship to come.

You once had strong, productive, and rich interactions on a certain basis. It went wrong. Without correction it will be lost for good, or very diminished. This resolution conversation is to put it back on track. The purpose of this step is to clearly state what 'on track' is.

Write down all the roles and links you have to each other, including ties you have at work, as friends, at home, out in the world. Most relationships begin on one basis and flower out into other dimensions. It's sometimes surprising the variety of ways you interact with each other. Capture all these connections; there are usually several, **one of which is the true nexus for this talk**. When you set them all out plainly this way, you may 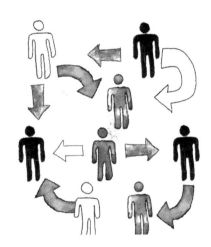 see where they overlap or conflict, and cause some trouble.

Next, go back and add some color to the list – specific detail about the purpose, range, and scope of each role. Give character to the relationship and describe what made it work well in the past.

It's important to be crisp, clean, and clear in your descriptions. Throwaways like, "I'm your buddy." won't cut it. And steer clear of embroidery. If you dress up your role descriptions to your advantage, or if you build up your own importance, it'll come back to bite you. You'll break the tie-in you're trying to re-establish. Same with minimization. If this wasn't an important linkage, you wouldn't be going to this trouble.

Once you've got the raw material, use it to shape your opening statement – the one that will kick off the discussion. Review the parts of your relationship and how they worked well before. Practice saying these things out loud. Now make it conversational; imagine your VIP nodding along as you speak…

David starts out

"Leonora, I'm on the line to deliver all the product commitments that Marketing dictates. They tell me what's needed to meet demand and then it's up to me to deliver. They're not interested in knowing what it takes to do it; they just want the product.

Your part in this is to arrange for everything we need from outside to the plant and to get it in position to be used in the production process.

That means no hitches. So, we buffer our supplies a bit to make sure that once we get going, there isn't even a hint of doubt there's going to be enough for the run.

I rely on you to do that, and then to get the product away to market. I count on you. I don't want to be looking over your shoulder or second-guessing. I want to have total confidence that everything will get done."

A point on Flow

You're not looking for dialogue to settle each point in turn. You don't seek agreement at this stage. In the moment, you make your statement, then move on. Once you have the ball rolling, you'll have settled both of you into your seats, facing forward together on your journey.

Your roles recollected, you can head out on the next leg of the trip – the facts.

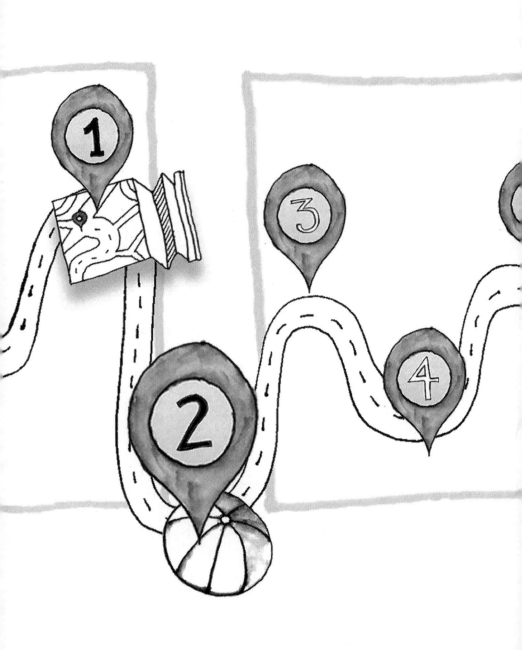

Step 2
The facts; your bumpy road

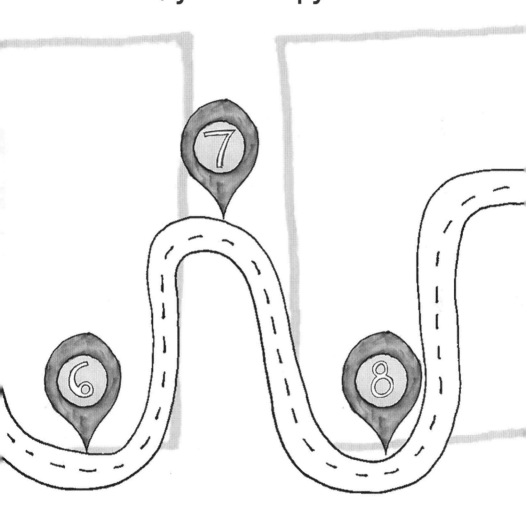

The Resolution Protocol

STEP 1   Describe your role and relationship
          to the other person.

STEP 2   **Outline the facts of a single incident
          that led to the relationship break.**

STEP 3   Express your emotional reaction to the
          situation and its impact on your identity.

STEP 4   Declare your part in creating or
          continuing the situation.

STEP 5   Listen to *their* version of what happened,
          and *their* emotional reaction.

STEP 6   Describe your expectations of what
          is required to set matters right.

STEP 7   Negotiate a path forward to
          rectify the situation.

STEP 8   Clarify your new agreement, and affirm
          your restored common purpose.

Step 1 is complete – you have clarified your roles and relationship with your VIP. When you get to the real talk, you have a reliable means to get started, set a positive tone, and orient both of you to the desired outcome.

Next, you lay out how your selected single incident unfolded. Step 2 again requires you to use crisp, clean, and clear language. Your VIP will have their own view of how things transpired. And they will have their chance to lay it out for you after Step 4.

This is your recitation of the facts. Include only the barebones. Strip out any self-serving gloss, embellishing thoughts, speculations, protective justifications, or personal conclusions. They're not facts. These unwanted elements are going to get in the way. They're easy to see and remove as you're prepping. We'll get to the emotions raised by the incident later.

Typically, unschooled people attempt to hammer out their disagreements using a courtroom model. This legal style is so deeply entrenched in our culture that it's reflexive – our 'go to' mode for dispute handling and very hard to get away from.

The trouble with 'courtroom' style

The courtroom is an arena for a fight conducted by **case building**. Trials work like this:

- The plaintiff brings out *all* the favorable details of their case. Then they present argument – *all* the reasons why they are in the right and the other is wrong.

- The defence lays out their version, which paints them in the most favorable light, and defuses the plaintiff's case.
- All this is done for the benefit of a judge, who hears this point-counterpoint recital and makes a final determination. Final until the appeal, of course…

Most disputants play 'courtroom'. They deploy slanted versions, justifications, evasions, denials, coloring of conduct and wily tactics to enhance their story, avoid responsibility, and cast blame on their adversary. They may even try to show bad intent behind the scenes. The tone is inflammatory and oppositional. And ultimately pointless. After all, there's no judge in the mix to determine who's right!

In your experience, is the courtroom style effective in resolving differences? I have yet to see the recipient of such an onslaught suddenly give up, confess all their wrongs, accept blame, be ashamed and act contrite. Instead, when the accuser stacks up their biased *proofs* of wrongdoing of the other, and uses ploys to trap the other party in a corner, the result is usually growing resentment and anger, or even revenge plots. The possibility of reconciliation becomes remote. Any path forward is obscured and the parties are thwarted from working *together* to resolve their differences.

The courtroom approach runs totally counter to an authentic resolution effort. The entire purpose of resolution is to bring estranged people *together* to work things out. It needs competent, composed players, not fragmented, inflamed antagonists. As the discussion progresses, it becomes clearer that both parties honestly want to stop pointless arguing, and get on the same page. The aim in resolution is for parties to take responsibility for all parts of the problem, and to voluntarily do what is necessary to put it right.

Here, the Protocol and the Mindset work together to avoid situations where combatants come out from their corners, swinging to win. Resolution is an arena for reconciliation.

Just the facts

In Step 2, you describe the incident in a way that adds to the foundation of mutual understanding you started building in Step 1. How? Remain focused on your selected **single incident**. Avoid the temptation to mention other events. Present the information in a chronological **time sequence**, and **stick to the facts.**

In this respect the Resolution Protocol does borrow something important from the legal world. The law of evidence is very specific about what constitutes a reliable, verifiable *fact:*

- What you said
- What they said to you
- What you both heard together
- What was written, can be pointed to, or produced

You too should stay within those guidelines... the same criteria used to admit evidence in a courtroom.

These are the tests your recitation of the incident must meet. Done well, your recap should seem a bit dry. The goal is for your VIP to stay with you as you tell the story. When you relate the incident in this controlled way, they are very likely to nod as you go along, saying, "Yes, that's right. That's what happened." You give them nothing to argue about.

Facts are not...

- Hearsay – anything anyone else said about the situation, other than what was said directly by you, or came from the other party, or was heard by you both.
- Speculations – assuming intentions or motives (*"That's when I thought you had it in for me."*)
- Suppositions, inferences, or conclusions – uncertain or incorrect beliefs (*"You had to know what they meant, just then."* or, *"I knew you didn't want that!"* or, *"When you did that, it was over."*)
- Justifications – self-serving rationalizations supporting how you acted (*"I was only trying to..."*)

If you include any hearsay, speculations, suppositions, inferences, conclusions, or justifications, you'll see your VIP's hackles rise instantly. The nodding will stop – a reliable sign they've gone crossways with you. If that happens and you don't interrupt your onrushing version of the story, you will lose them. There will be no point in continuing.

> ⚠ Add anything but facts and you block working together. You'll feel it necessary to include all sorts of extra information, but it will only throw your talk off course. Next chapter you'll learn a way to keep yourself on track, as we get into the Relationship Guidance System.

Your whole purpose is to take great care as you refill a still-fragile trust bucket, and prevent it from breaking again. If you persist in the face of their disagreement, you will no longer be advancing your mission together.

Sticking to the facts may be really difficult. All this speculating, justifying, and supposing has been churning within
you for a long time! Second-guessing the other person's
motives, intent, or fact bases – gleaned from sparse clues –
has fueled your ruminations. Divesting yourself of all this
emotional baggage may be challenging, but sticking to the
facts of a single incident will clear the way to resolving the
conflict. Be grateful that the emotional charge has given
you the impetus to initiate this talk.

Beach ball

No two people see a situation the same way.

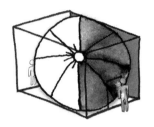

Imagine a room that's completely filled – floor
to ceiling, wall to wall – with a giant inflated,
bi-colored beach ball. Two doors, on opposite
walls, open onto the room.

If you ask the person opening one door what's
inside, they will say "A giant red ball! Fills the whole room."

Ask the person opening the other door and they'll say...well,
you get it. Both looks are correct, but neither has a lock on
a precise description of what is in that room. Each person's
perception is their truth.

Let's get further into David's conversation with Leonora as
he tackles Step 2 concerning the stock-out that jeopardized
a production run at Dugmore Foods.

David describes the facts to Lenora this way:

"Lenora, we were both at the Operations Forum last Wednesday. Sally and Fernando were with us in the second-floor boardroom. On the agenda was the production run for one of the cookie lines. Do you recall?"

"Yes..."

David sees Leonora's body language change, stiffening a bit.

"Fernando introduced the readiness checklist for the run. When he got to the part where he mentioned ingredient quantities, you said, 'There may be an issue with almond flour.'"

"Yes...I did."

"Then I noticed Sally lean forward. And I saw you grimace..."

Notice how David just reports exactly what happened. He is specific and literal. Leonora is looking hard at him, but nodding...

Map it out

Creating a timeline is an ideal way to lay out your incident. Begin with a horizontal line; the start of the incident sits at the far left, and the ending goes at the far right. Place distinct date/time points along the line to mark the order of events as they occurred. Make notes near the points with the details.

It is also helpful to establish the context. Set up the scene where the incident occurred – time, location, atmosphere. That's typically pretty easy to agree with! 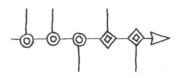 Also include whatever factual information is needed to put you both in a shared picture, without belaboring or minimizing any element. Reciting the rest of the incident may go quickly, in the form of dialogue. *I said, then you said, then we went...* Often there's been an exchange that proved damning.

Preparing to describe the incident may produce some surprises – relevant interactions you've overlooked or forgotten, or particular turning points that take on greater significance. You may need to extend your timeline's start/end points as your memory sharpens.

Facts are a safe haven. They help both of you **get on the same page about what happened.** Exploring the impacts of it all will come soon.

Even as you work through this recall assignment, change is afoot. Step 2 preparation makes you look differently at the incident and your VIP. Being able to put your finger on the exact circumstances of the trust breach allows you to touch on your bruised nerve and notice how it affected you. You're starting to become *unstuck*, letting you begin moving on. It's all part of the process.

You might feel this is getting quite involved! It's for a good reason. The Protocol asks you to be disciplined and stick to the structure. The payoff is release! So don't give up. It will be okay, I promise.

Enough background. Add the events and factual details to the timeline on your Preparation Worksheet – enough so your VIP can follow along with you. Ditch any extra stuff that will throw them off. There – Step 2 preparation complete.

After a brief rest stop with the following chapter to learn more about how to navigate, we'll get back in the car for Step 3 on your journey to wholeness.

Rest stop! A guidance system for a turbulent ride

"Why would I subject myself and others to this discomfort given everything that's on our plate?" Because what's on the other side of your most frustrating relationships is worth it: relief, success, health, freedom from stress, happiness, a high-performing team, a fulfilling personal relationship."

— *SUSAN SCOTT*

The ball is rolling now, following your review of the facts. You're over the initial jitters but about to hit some loose gravel on the road.

This interlude between Steps 2 and 3 is given to some vital skill-building that will help you keep your head, while showing your heart. Call it a rest stop on this resolution journey; you'll spend a bit of time here, learning how to keep the conversation on track.

To direct your talk productively, you will use a device I call the Resolution Guidance System (RGS) to:

- Move the discussion deliberately to its destination, and
- Avoid treacherous territory that can derail the two of you.

The RGS is a navigational tool that helps you spot if your chat strays off course, then recover.

Recall where all this is going. You decided to face up to a difficult situation with someone you care about. Even though you're apprehensive, you want to reach nothing less than **full and complete resolution** of the fracture that divided you. That's your destination, your purpose.

You're likely to face some difficult driving on the road ahead. Heavy weather is forecast, and the cross-traffic may be hard to handle as you confront and deal with long-held, highly charged differences. This trip will test your composure and determination. You'll be tempted to veer away or stop short of your goal. But nevertheless, you've decided this is worth it. Your regard for your VIP and your connection supplies courage to brave the potential emotional storms. The further along you get, the more momentum aids you.

I urge you to steer forward, be guided by informed intuition, using the RGS. It helps keep your ego out of the driver's seat!

Imagine if the pilot of your Big Apple bound airplane announced, *"We're going to try to go to New York..."*

Or, if your car-share driver said, *"I'll do my best to get you to Grand Central Station, but no promises..."*

What?? Wouldn't you get the urge to scram? You want them to take you *all* the way there!

Sensible drivers or pilots use guidance systems to help them reach their goal, particularly over unfamiliar ground.

The automotive industry offers multiple onboard guidance systems: a GPS that shows your current location and the route onward; lane departure sensors, anti-collision braking mechanisms, blind-spot alerts... All these keep the driver and passengers safe, despite possible distraction or inattention. They help keep a vehicle centered in its lane, away from dangerous circumstances, and headed in the right direction.

Likewise, **you** need suitable navigational aids to stay safely on course. You need to be alerted to potential hazards, and be guided back if you happen to take a wrong turn. You need a GPS – in our case the RGS – to detect your error... *recalculating...*

The good news is you **already possess** an inherent guidance system to help you steer true. This capacity is in-built, but you may not have given it a label, or had to rely on it so clearly before.

The Resolution Guidance System (RGS)

The RGS visualizes your trajectory and alerts you to deviations. You use it to keep a difficult talk away from risky terrain, and to home in on your goal.

People get pretty activated in these heavy talks. They show many less-than-admirable, unhelpful behaviors and states of mind that can wreak havoc. Isn't the potential for that why you're apprehensive?

When people are animated in the line of fire, they instinctively rely on these tactics. Anger- or fear-based behaviors were born under extremely heated circumstances. They worked back then to divert away from hard topics - to prevail over, or avoid difficult people or cases.

Let's talk through how anger or fear manifests in a spicy talk.

Anger	Fear
displays as	*displays as*
• Erupting	• Making nice
• Yelling	• Avoidance
• Sarcasm	• Sloughing off [everything is fine] *John K.*
• Arguing	*called this 'dung shining'*
• Lashing out	• Minimizing [not that big a deal]
• Glowering	• Manipulating
• Manipulating	• Going blank [spacing out]
• Bullying	• Indifference [silent, impassive]
• Attacking	• Crying and emoting
	• Smoothing over

No doubt you've experienced (or used) some reactions on this list in past heated interactions. Look to the Appendix for a more extensive list. These responses are ignited by the survival-oriented primitive brain. Operating subconsciously, and activated by anything seen to be a threat or a chance to *go get 'em*, your brain floods a body and mind with hormones that scream *Fight! Kill! Escape!*

Nothing said or heard in a difficult conversation *actually* presents physical danger, but our primal brain responds as if it were a threat or opportunity for advantage. If these mostly involuntary behaviors manifest in either of you, you'll take a wrong turn and shift focus away from your intent to sensitively get to the heart of the matter.

But hey! You should expect reactions! This talk *should* activate your counterpart. Strong emotions and inertia have kept you stuck in stubborn positions. Don't rise to the bait if your VIP gets jacked up. As if that shouldn't occur. You hit a nerve! That's success!

Either one of you could make moves stirred up by the subconscious. And if you're not on top of your resolution game, you'll find yourself pushed out of your lane and headed for the ditch. Without quick correction, you'll no longer be driving to your destination. You need the RGS.

The RGS inside

I want you to install a mental RGS gauge. In challenging wayfinding, you want it to pop up the instant you sense a tell-tale reaction.

A warning light should flare on the left side of the gauge if you experience aggressive, anger-based behaviors. Similarly, an alert should flash on the right side when you see withdrawing, fear-based behaviors. No matter their source, if these signals are not addressed right away, you'll veer off the road.

What force pulls you back to center?

In Canada, Beaver Cubs are an organization for little kids, aged five to seven, that's part of the Scouting movement. At the opening of their meetings the leader calls out "Riverbanks!", and the eager young faces race to sit on the floor, facing each other in two lines. The leader calls out, "What do we do?" And in one loud voice the Beaver Cubs shout back, "Sharing, Sharing. Sharing!" That's their rallying cry.

Ours is Caring! Caring! Caring!

Sounds corny and old-fashioned to say it that way. Calling up a mental mantra is a superb centering tactic to use when you're rocked. It's a strategy that's been around for a long time. There's nothing technologically advanced about it. A mantra interrupts your urge to react with anger or fear. With one word, you engage your higher brain, recall why you are in this conversation at all, and your 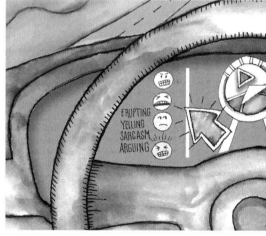 defenses settle down. This causes your RGS indicator to swing back to center, and you find the appropriate words – they come from your heart.

The second you find yourself activated during the conversation (and you should expect it), you've got to interrupt yourself. How do you do that? The activation flashes a warning on your RGS as you're talking. Your gut reactions will fire first: *Fight this! Get out of here! Calm them down!* But that's not for you. Your higher functioning brain notices the flash of upset. You very deliberately repeat that *Caring! Caring! Caring!* mantra inside. And it settles you down; allows you room to straighten matters out.

I know I've gone on a bit about 'caring'. For good reason. It is indispensable to this work. Your approach must be anchored and animated by the care you have for your VIP. None of this works if it is not in service to your regard for them.

Even if your reason is primarily for business, go deep and get that caring basis out where you can see it. Center yourself on it.

Having trouble finding it? Look no further than the regret that impelled you to get serious about this work. That's it. Get clear on your caring before going any further. And make that the biggest thing in your sphere.

The RGS is the indispensable tool for this reorientation process. It acts like a combination GPS and lane departure sensor, and gets you through the danger zones. It signals whether you're on track – centered in your lane, going in the right direction – or not.

Earlier, you learned that as the initiator of this conversation, you take on the job of stewarding its Flow. It's in this capacity that you also **neutralize diverting behaviors**.

You monitor the back-and-forth and so long as you are both driving toward resolution, your heads-up RGS Gauge indicates that you're lined up true, and exactly on course. But if an alert fires because either of one of you has a reaction, the RGS pops up. Before your mind can even process the situation, your instincts tell you to adjust.

You deter primitive responses by interrupting your impulse. It's like calling a friend for help on a quiz show. You ask your developed brain to help you steer back on course. When I say this RGS system is in-built, this is what I mean. You already possess this balancing capability, and if you use it well, it leads you true.

A little farther along in this book, I take you into body sensibility. For now, it's useful to know that even before you see primal reactions, you have *another* in-built capacity to notice earlier and more subtle clues about what is happening within your VIP or yourself. The body is always speaking. Watch the other person carefully; you'll see if you tread too close to their boundaries. The minute you touch on a hypersensitive topic, or you go too fast/slow for them to stay with you, you'll see your VIP's discomfort reflected in an involuntary physical reaction. When you learn more about body-language signals, you'll find them easy to pick up, and another excellent way to monitor the undercurrents of your conversation.

Creating the ability for your VIP to **track with you** is a hallmark of this process. Throughout a thorny talk, your continuous awareness of your VIP's boundaries ensures they remain in sync with you. You also monitor and adjust your own reactions – body and mind.

With your senses feeding in data and your RGS monitoring the action, you'll find you are more calm and better able to deal constructively with whatever happens. You'll rise to the occasion.

The practical RGS

How does this unfold in real life? As you conduct the conversation, have the *RGS on a Page* in hand (from the Appendix or *DougBouey.com/ffdownloads*), and keep it front of mind. Use all your *spidey senses* when you head into sensitive territory. Continually evaluate the situation to detect adverse reactions, and assess their vectors – anger or fear. Be ready for alerts to flare left or right on your RGS gauge.

Your intuition will tell you if you touch a live wire. Even if you must pause a moment when the spark hits you (in the turmoil of your own emotions), take time to recenter on your purpose. Call on your higher self to intervene (Caring, Caring, Caring). Then use counter-measures that come from your heart to alter the direction of the conversation.

It can be as simple as putting up your hands and saying, "whoa!"

Now, let's look in again on David and Leonora in that second-floor boardroom.

David has traversed the roles in the previous excerpt and has already started in on Step 2, the facts.

With tension rising in the room, David hits a nerve.

"You shuffled a few reports, looked down and muttered something about a shortfall."

Leonora sits sat up straight and stares at David with eyes of fire.

"I said there's a chance we will be short. And I didn't mutter, as you put it. I said it clear, and the others heard me."

David, live to the sensitivity, looks down at his Worksheet.

"I hope you don't mind but I put some advance thoughts down here... And you're right. It was certainly clear there was an issue."

He continues reciting the facts.

"Then you said, 'We may be short on almond flour.'"

I asked, "How short?" and you said, 'About 300 pounds.'"

"That's right," agrees Leonora, her shoulders dropping a bit.

"And that's when Fernando said, 'What we've got should last until tomorrow afternoon, if we start tonight.'"

And I said, "Well, that's a real problem. We'll have to stop short. Not enough run for packaging."

"Yep. Not a happy moment." says Leonora, looking aside and down.

David winds up his list of facts with, "And then you excused yourself, saying you had to make a couple of calls. And, somehow, a delivery arrived the next day at noon, and we made the run."

"We did…" says Leonora, breathing out, and reengaging with David.

David and Leonora's episode is a fairly typical early resolution exchange. Although David is firmly in the Initiator's role and directing the Flow, he uses his RGS wisdom, slows down, and gives himself time to make a correction. Although obviously disturbed, Leonora, stays with him. How does he pull that off?

Despite the rising tension, David steers true, even though he senses that Leonora might be ready to attack. He doesn't waver, but neither does he move hard.

As he senses Leonora bristling, he realizes he has mischaracterized Leonora by using the word *muttered,* and it has inflamed her. The conversation heads for the ditch! He recognizes that her reaction is an Anger warning signal, and it silently speaks volumes: *Careful, there…you're putting words in my mouth and I know the stakes here…*

David adjusts, unapologetically refers to his notes, perhaps consults his RGS on a Page to center the needle, and it works. He doesn't back away, but is more respectful and repeats her exact words.

Leonora is an essential part of the Dugmore team. He doesn't want to lose her, cause unwanted family disruption, or for anything to get in the way of her good work, but he still has to get his point across.

It can take so little to upset the applecart. Just putting a gloss, a little too much color on a comment can be enough to get yourself crossways with your VIP.

But it's not so tough to navigate. Just read the gauge – which for David is echoed by his own body's apprehension – and *shift*. Do anything but get full of yourself and *let 'er rip!* You know that David could have said, "Yeah, you did too mutter. I know evasion when I see it! And I wanted the straight goods, right then and there!" That would surely have led to disaster.

David hasn't come all this way to have that kind of train wreck. There is no percentage in that, and the momentary consolation his ego will relish will be pretty cold comfort if the company has to scour the streets for a high-performing logistics VP on short notice. Not with product demand at an all time high... and the CEO coming down his throat about needlessly upsetting...well... everything, as the collateral damage hits the fan.

The RGS is yours to use anytime (not just in a resolution conversation). It immediately reads mind/body reactions, and signals when you're headed away from your objective. Focus on your care and respect for the other party, and you'll stay on course, keeping the other person with you every step of the way.

Seems like a lot, but it's not

First, I asked you to follow a structured process, the Resolution Protocol. Then to ground yourself in the Relationship Mindset to secure your attitude and orientation. Now, as you prepare, and later as you talk together, I ask you to infuse your attention with the Resolution Guidance System.

I assure you this isn't difficult – in fact it's very straight-forward. The Mindset brought you here in the first place. And the RGS already exists, built into the exquisitely sensate human being that you are. So you simply tap into a higher state of awareness. And that's okay too, because you're already hyper-sensitized (nervous!). All you need to do is channel the information received in your activated state through to the RGS, and it will convert it to signals that help you steer straight to the heart of the issue.

Thanks for bearing with me. This chapter is so central to the approach, it demands this extra attention. I'm glad you didn't skip it. It's an extremely worthwhile investment in yourself.

The heart of the fracture is usually embedded in the emotional lair. It holds the present situation in traction. Let's go on to Step 3, please!

You're in the driver's seat, and heading into sensitive territory… your emotional reactions to the incident, and its impacts on your identity.

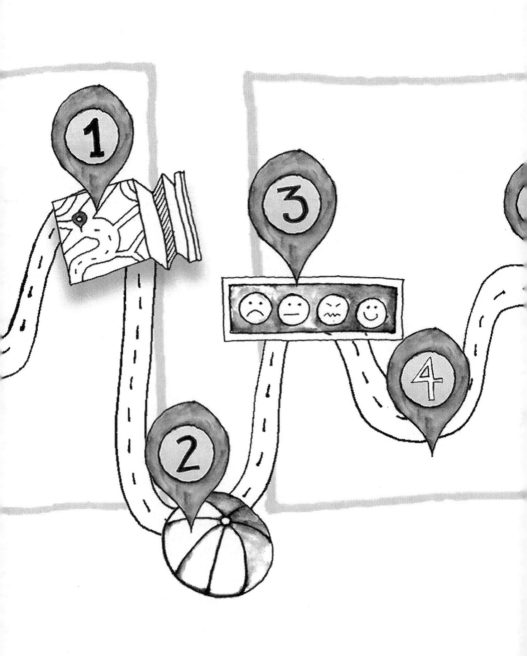

Step 3

The driver; emotions and identity

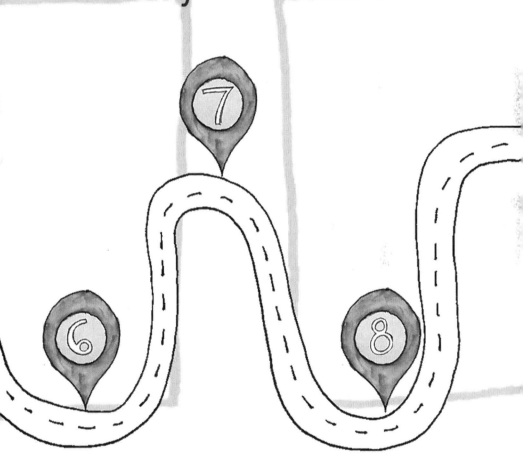

The Resolution Protocol

STEP 1   Describe your role and relationship to the other person.

STEP 2   Outline the facts of a single incident that led to the relationship break.

STEP 3   **Express your emotional reaction to the situation and its impact on your identity.**

STEP 4   Declare your part in creating or continuing the situation.

STEP 5   Listen to *their* version of what happened, and *their* emotional reaction.

STEP 6   Describe your expectations of what is required to set matters right.

STEP 7   Negotiate a path forward to rectify the situation.

STEP 8   Clarify your new agreement, and affirm your restored common purpose.

> *"Say it straight, or*
> *you'll show it crooked!"*

— ABE WAGNER

You've traversed the facts of the incident, and now share a base from which to move forward. You have the Resolution Guidance System in hand to steady you in this (or any) loaded situation.

But your own troubled state of affairs is made up of more than just facts. Emotions are a big part of it. To close in on the crux of the matter, you need to say and know more.

The Protocol's disciplined approach structures an orderly discussion of *all* the elements that make up your unique mess. Here in Step 3, you advance the resolution process by disclosing your feelings – the emotions this incident aroused. Even though people worry that emotions will consume any vexing discussion, the Protocol gives them their proper place – right here.

Situations you'd rather forget always have significant feelings attached. And they are hard to straighten out precisely because they are powder

kegs. The reactions triggered by your incident have detonated a breach of trust. To rescue your valued relationship, these hurt feelings must be aired; they cannot be ignored. Withheld anger, disappointment, fear, false hope – whatever you've got – here's where you give them voice.

Many people avoid raising sensitive issues because they fear losing competence in the grasp of uncontrollable feelings – their own or those of others. This reticence is justified. Emotions have you; you don't have them. They swamp logic and muddle thinking.

I can assure you that Step 3 won't be the flood-fest you fear. You will reveal your feelings, but you'll also be able to stay in your in your lane, steady through any unexpected reactions to your disclosure.

You both need to know how to name the feelings that have affected you. Only then can they take their appropriate place – *not* in the driver's seat of this conversation. Once they're out on the table, they lose their special power and both of you feel more settled.

None of this is done to *fix* anyone's emotions.

By bringing emotions to light, you provide useful information to your VIP so they understand your state. You lose any sense that you're a helpless victim being held hostage, or that you're a bullying tyrant yourself. And usually, both parties feel more *grown up* as a result – they are real people confronting events of consequence. Emotion is how humans experience significance, after all.

A word about reaction patterns

People sometimes try to anticipate emotional actions and reactions, commonly by relying on stereotypes. Do you think that women tend to be immersed in emotions and men deny or repress them? In my sessions I sometimes find that to be true. It's difficult to get men to voice their feelings, or stem the tide when women flood. And sometimes it's the reverse!

Regardless of stereotypes, we each have particular and largely subconscious ways to express overwhelming emotion. Dare I say it's how our immaturity creeps in, tries to take over, and skews rationality around minefield issues.

Without becoming an amateur shrink, you can take note of the apparent emotional age in a reaction. Coping mechanisms develop in our early years. The more intense an encounter, the more likely a patterned, regressive response will emerge. At a certain level of heat, an otherwise controlled person might suddenly snap, drop their veneer of unruffled disinterest, and want to duke it out. Other times, you can be facing a six-year-old in a schoolyard, overwrought and lost. In difficult conversations, someone might lunge at the other, or storm out slamming the door, or break down sobbing as the talk nears a telling point.

That's okay! It's where they are. It shows the significance of what's being discussed in that moment. Reactions are not innately *wrong* or *bad* (unless of course they are violent and harmful). They are information – the effect of an interaction that shows how close to the bone impact was felt. If you can call upon your caring, you may be able to empathize with them in their distress.

All yours

For the other person to *really get* the impact the incident has had, state the feelings that had hold of you. Later, you'll solicit your VIP's side, but for now it's just about you.

⚠ *Never describe your emotions by saying, "I felt that..." Using this phrase is a cloaked attempt at manipulation. That is not a feeling. That introduces a conclusion (what was expected, should have happened, or been true). If you say I felt that..., you'll put your VIP off. They'll stop tracking with you. They'll sense a set-up in the making, and they don't want that. You don't either.*

You continue to lead the discussion by describing your incident-related emotions. And only yours. How?

You use *feeling* words, first on your Preparation Worksheet, then in person: *I felt... I was... my feelings about that were...* State them all, and out loud. Don't short-circuit yourself by minimizing them, pretending they weren't central, or that they didn't hold you in their grip.

Then most importantly, put feelings right where they belong. At the end of your recitation, you must always add this critical phrase:

"...**and those are mine to deal with.**"

Here's how David tells Leonora about his feelings:

"Leonora, when you said we were close to shorting out supply at our meeting, my heart just sank. I was so disappointed, then mad, and so upset that I just couldn't speak. I went silent. And those feelings are mine to deal with."

It's clear to Leonora that David is only talking about himself. And David isn't presuming to guess or express Leonora's internal state.

FIXING FRACTURES

How could anyone know what others feel? You're not a mind-reader, and cannot speak for others. If you say, "*I know you must be feeling…*", you're certain to rankle your VIP. That doesn't mean they aren't affected by what you say. They'll have their own reactions to report in due course. **And those are theirs to deal with.**

In the Protocol, emotions are never tools for manipulation; that would impair resolution. Go back and have a look at the RGS gauge… *manipulating* appears on both the Fear and Anger sides of the chart.

Now, all emotions are variants of *mad / sad / glad / scared.* I often hear words like *disappointed, upset,* and *surprised* when participants want to blunt the impact of the rawer emotion they really felt. Many people not only have difficulty stating feelings precisely, but don't like expressing them at all. They aren't used to that level of exposure and vulnerability. But how will you resolve your situation if you stay behind your walls?

> Some people have devious motives for expressing their feelings in a hard conversation. They may have had success using feelings – which others may recoil from – to get results. They may want to incite sympathy so they're let off the hook. They may 'work the feelings angle' to get what they want, or pressure another into letting them win. These ploys must have got them what they wanted at some early point in their emotional development. So, as the temperature of a conversation rises, they regress and go back to their gimmick.

To help get past this hesitancy, you can consult the Emotions Wheel. It's an accepted tool that originated with American psychologist Dr. Robert Plutchik to help people pinpoint words that describe their emotions. You can find lots of examples and good information about the Emotions Wheel online. Use it as you complete your Preparation Worksheet to select the exact right words to describe your feelings. Be as direct as you can in your conversation; don't forget the crucial phrase… *and those are mine to deal with.*

Most people worry about disclosing their emotions; they wonder if they'll alienate their VIP. In most cases, Initiators find that their hidden feelings created distance. By expressing emotions, you bring the other person closer. In *Fierce Conversations,* Susan Scott confirms, "When you offer up your true self, others will recognize it and respond."

The punch line, *"and those are mine to deal with"*, makes it clear to your VIP that they don't have to *do anything* in particular about what they hear. Of course, when you reveal your emotions, you make it obvious that you don't plan to linger there. Your Step 3 mission is simply to make the impact of events known.

Beyond emotion to identity

Difficult incidents have impact – the magnitude is measured by depth of feeling. But difficult incidents have another, even more troublesome aspect. Either or both of the involved parties can believe they have been reduced in standing, or made to feel less than who they believe they are, at their core.

We each cherish elements of our status. They are parts of our identity, and assure us of our position, our significance as contributing people. If you think of yourself as, say, a good parent, a competent professional, a solid partner, or a worthy friend, you'll be deeply offended by any suggestions to the contrary.

Frequently in fractured relationships, identities have been slighted by a comment or inference made during the incident. It hits near to the core of who the players believe themselves to be. It's a big part of how we make our way in the world. Defenses go way up and reaction to the mischaracterization is highly charged.

Was your identity injured? You need to say it.

In the Preparation Worksheet, there's a spot for you to identify such impacts. What did this incident say about the ideals of self you hold most dear? Did you feel disrespected in a capacity you're proud of? Write it down and get it out.

Whew! After you get through Step 3 in your talk, you'll probably feel relieved. It's a remarkable moment when you finally voice your feelings to your VIP, and they are still in the room, still in their seat. The feared eruption has (generally) not occurred. Frequently, the other party is surprised at the emotional and identity impacts of the incident; they just didn't know. Theirs may be stirred up.

This is information your VIP needs so they can move forward with you toward resolution. When the full context is known, every reaction makes perfect sense.

With your emotions now on the table, the tone of the conversation shifts, goes deeper. The Protocol gives this information its proper place, so nobody gets lost in a firestorm of feelings. The impact of the incident is simply another element in a complex picture; no longer the whole story. Your VIP will have a chance to express their feelings too. Soon.

Our journey takes us next over a bridge that spans a deep chasm where your very own trolls reside. You come face to face with why this unique approach to resolving difference is so effective. The big bridge has a name: 100% → 0% Accountability.

Step 4

Over the bridge; take radical ownership

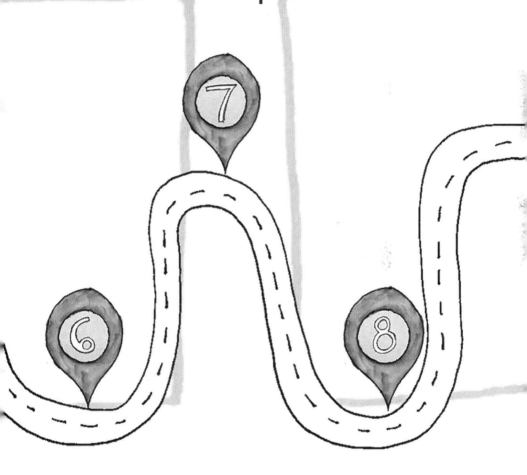

The Resolution Protocol

STEP 1   Describe your role and relationship
          to the other person.

STEP 2   Outline the facts of a single incident
          that led to the relationship break.

STEP 3   Express your emotional reaction to the
          situation and its impact on your identity.

**STEP 4   Declare your part in creating
          or continuing the situation.**

STEP 5   Listen to *their* version of what happened,
          and *their* emotional reaction.

STEP 6   Describe your expectations of what
          is required to set matters right.

STEP 7   Negotiate a path forward to
          rectify the situation.

STEP 8   Clarify your new agreement, and affirm
          your restored common purpose.

"How come every time I get stabbed in the back, my finger-prints are on the knife?"

– JERRY HARVEY

Now that the incident and its impacts are on the table, you are well into the talk. Keep going. You are about to make the last of the Initiator's opening declarations.

It may feel odd that you hold center stage for so long. Remember this is purposeful – it's part of the Flow, the structured organization of the conversation.

In modern discussions, people are fixated on the idea of securing *permission* to proceed beyond each material statement. No one speaks for a sustained period of time; it's a familiar and comforting to-and-fro. This habit also keeps discussion light, shallow and narrow, less penetrating. Initiators sometimes sense they are way out on a limb, without those regular validations, affirmations, or replies. It's just not their *style*. Well, get over it. This is no ordinary coffee shop chat.

Following Step 3's revelations of the impacts, you've created an avenue to further openness. And now you take on your most elusive opponent – yourself.

Take a deep breath. You're headed onto that bridge over troubled waters, where you **take personal ownership for everything** that caused this situation. You read that right. You will take complete responsibility for how this regrettable incident began and has continued. You will leave none of the responsibility on your VIP's shoulders. You caused it. Totally.

100% you → 0% them

It's called *radical ownership,* and dramatic movement to your destination demands it.

John Konstanturos' innovative **100%→0% Accountability** declaration opens the gates to resolution. He first used this method to defuse the volatile Los Angeles Watts riots in the 1960s. Back then, application of the 100%→0% Accountability model drove a massive reduction in tensions. Reconciliation was achieved between violent *factions,* not just individuals. Now it will work for you.

When people learn of this requirement, most want to stand down, get off the bridge, stop the music, take a pass. They fight it tooth-and-nail.

"What do you mean, I did it all? You must be kidding!"

People are proud. Most of us feel we are generally upstanding, proper-thinking, solid citizens. Well, despite that, something has gone wrong here! Yes, you generally do right in the world. But if you believe you are always correct in every respect, I doubt you'd still be reading this!

I'm being something of a smart ass now. You decided to take a risk to deal with a severe difference. You have taken steps to learn, grow, explore new insights and alternatives. Those moves acknowledge an unfinished self, with room to progress along the road to becoming someone better. And you can't get better if you think you're already perfect.

Your ego is hugely invested in *keeping you right*, and as a result holds you in a very poor place. It wants to protect your self-esteem, prevent you from hurt, be vindicated... even if it is only to yourself. It speaks to you endlessly, directs your actions, bolsters your confidence in your *correctness* – past and present. You know that commentator in your ear always voicing judgments about others and directing you about what you're encountering? That's it.

The ego hates the whole 100%→0% idea. It will resolutely rebel, and try to hobble your natural human capacity to rise above differences and get past difficulties.

Under its influence, you expect certain behaviors and actions from others and yourself, and you also edit your past sins out of memory. This is all so you can function, and don't always flounder in a sea of doubt.

The incident emptied your trust bucket with your VIP, and hurt your feelings. Those emotions and broken expectations activated your ego... *'this is wrong!'* Since the incident, it has defended your position and prevented you from changing how you perceive or interact with your VIP. It has increased the distance between the two of you 'to protect you', and erected defences against any kind of repeat.

Here in Step 4, you put aside all this self-comforting assurance **and stop blaming others**.

Now you revisit the incident and take responsibility for every part of how it unfolded and turned out.

It is *not* phony playacting or a clever trick. It's real. And when you complete the Preparation Worksheet for this step, you will begin to appreciate just how true it is... *that you did it all.* You had many, many opportunities to handle this better.

You'll also come to see this is the only way to acquire the power to alter your circumstances. So long as you believe it's up to the other person to fix this mess (because it's all *their* fault), is just how long you'll stay stuck – waiting for them to do something.

Let's work through this tough notion a bit. In the past, when I laid the 100%→0% concept on a particular player in a deadlock, they said,

*"But how can that be? **They** were behind the whole thing!"*

Of course the other party has always had some part to play. But at this stage of the conversation, you'll only advance to resolution when you own the entire onset and continuation of the issue.

Rest assured you do not have to prostrate yourself, or absorb responsibility for *all* the other person's actions.

To each his own... role

And when I say that, I'm not giving your ego an out to escape from having to do this work. I mean that whatever you say in Step 4 must be consistent with the Initiator's appropriate role vis-a-vis the VIP.

Let's see how this works and sounds for David and Leonora:

David:

"Leonora this is not the first time I've been nervous about your part in timing supplies for production. That's my bad... I let it slide because we got through when you pulled off some heroic moves.

And I have to say that I let our family tie get in the way of telling you right out how I felt. I was afraid that someone else would get involved and we wouldn't be able to work it out ourselves.

But I didn't raise it with you afterward and get clear with you. I should have. That wasn't fair – my confidence in you had been damaged, and I didn't deal straight with you about that.

I also haven't ever told you how allergic I am to drama. I just can't stand last minute emergencies!

And I don't think I've ever asked you to give me a full presentation on your processes and alliances for supply, so I can fully understand how you run your department.

I guess I've just taken it all for granted, and that's not consistent with my proper oversight of the entire division."

100%→0% accountability admissions do not excuse bad conduct, or diminish the requirement for change

Pause a moment. Do you see how the structure of the Protocol starts to knit together now? Radical ownership, on your part, is based on how you described your roles and relationship in Step 1. You're working to restore or improve how you both get along in your roles going forward – a good boss, a caring friend, a more capable parent.

Woulda, Shoulda, Coulda

 This step is all about what was missed. Look hard in the rear-view mirror, and put your precious ego in a time-out. With the benefit of 20/20 hindsight, reach deep inside and identify your errors.

Let the words *woulda, shoulda,* and *coulda* make your preparation easier:

Woulda

If I turned back time and knew then what I know now, **I would have** thought more about potential problems. I *woulda* [done this…, said that…, been more…]. That way we wouldn't even be here.

Shoulda

I regret what transpired, and **I should have** done something different when there was still an opportunity to change what eventually happened. To head this off I *shoulda* [done this..., said that..., been less...]

Coulda

If I'd been a little more aware or sensitive, **I could have** played my hand differently before a bad situation got worse. I *coulda* [done this..., said that..., been better at...]

It's dramatic how much comes out, how different things could have been, how clearly you were offside, and how absolutely naked you feel when you see it so starkly. All this despite your ego's strident insistence that you did nothing wrong.

That's **100%→0%** in action. It's rigorous and unsparing. It sounds like weakness, but it's not. It's a show of inner strength and conviction that sets a much more open stage for the resolution to come.

Your VIP will love it, and lean into it. Their empathy may be activated and they may surprise you by taking a step toward resolution, saying something like, *"No, that wasn't only you..."*

Now, it's always best to err on the side of more accountability than less. You're human, so you'll miss some things. Even if their compassion is rising, your VIP may still be mired in the blame game, and be quick to top up your list! By the end of this talk, you can be sure you'll know every bit of how you caused or continued the issue.

Once you take full ownership, you and your VIP both understand that you're not going to make those errors again.

So, you take 100% accountability not to put yourself down, but for a greater purpose – to drive the conversation squarely to the heart of the issue. In no uncertain words, you show your capacity and willingness to go great lengths to put things right.

Snowball fight

A friend who learned this process once said,

"I just love this part!"

"Really? Most find it quite tough…"

"Nah! It's like being in a snowball fight. Just as we're warming up, I waltz over to their snow fort and take away all their snowballs.

Now I'm holding all the ammunition they would have used against me!"

With 100% of the responsibility on you, there's 0% left for your VIP. There's no reason to argue; you've taken all the blame. It's time for you both to deal.

Take out your Preparation Worksheet, and send your ego on recess. Review the sequence of events in your incident, then write out your part in all of it. Let the truth of *woulda / shoulda / coulda* start to break open the hardened crust over your breach of trust. Solvent has been added to the mix and the whole problem begins to dissolve into something more friendly...

You're safely across the bridge. Time to gas up and have a full tank for the next rousing and vital part of the road to resolution.

Pit stop! Amp up awareness; be ready to really listen

You are well on your way now, and over the most taxing of the Protocol steps, 100%→0% Accountability. Now we'll pause to take on a bit more fuel for Step 5 and beyond.

So far, you've had the *comfort* of doing all the talking. From here on, this chat will be mutual and more productive as a result. A heightened ability to observe and hear your VIP will help you interact fully, whether you stand strong or temporarily totter. In this chapter I focus less on preparation, and more on your own readiness to experience the actual conversation.

Certain fundamental points of view animate the Resolution Protocol. Early on you learned that the Protocol is a *program* you run to direct the discussion. And that it only runs on the correct *operating system* – the Relationship Mindset. In this Chapter we look at aspects of the Mindset that enable a successful resolution conversation:

- Framing difference
- Active listening
- Body sensibility

Maybe you've heard or know something about the elements on that list, and already agree that they're great practices. Perhaps you're considering skipping this chapter. Don't. I think when you read on, you'll find some fresh insight.

To now, you've initiated and led this tricky discussion, carefully articulated the roles, laid out matters of fact on a single issue, disclosed the impacts, and taken 100% accountability for a defining incident.

And as you progressed, you've become increasingly mindful, admitted your vulnerability, and opened yourself to what must unfold in order to reach resolution. It didn't just happen in your mind; you also felt it in your body. Likely, you're feeling some uneasiness; you just don't feel good. These stirrings are a positive thing; they're the music of your frame of reference shifting as you face into the encounter, and also the reawakening of conscience.

You are enhancing your **relational skills**. Your exposure to this process is rendering you more able to deal with *whatever* life throws at you. This work is developmental; it enlarges your sense of what's possible. You cannot help but grow personally when you:

- Learn how to effectively approach and engage someone who has a different, even challenging perspective;
- Take careful steps forward even when you are emotionally activated, to uncover and explore difficult issues;
- Venture with others into the unknown, to understand resistance, develop options, and commit to changes for outcomes that are better for everyone involved.

Difference is okay

You are dealing with a *difference.* You and your VIP are separate people, with unique abilities and contributions that brought you together in the first place. They also keep you in this jam.

Problems between people are *natural* – they happen all the time, simply because we are different from each other. Variety is essential to life; it's how change occurs, and how new things are created.

Recall the Relationship Mindset – it grounds your discussion in care and compassion for the other person. It underpins your commitment to set the situation right. Led by the Mindset, you help yourself and your VIP remain wholly present in the conversation, and able to interact effectively to reach resolution. And along the way, you move beyond the idea that difficulties between people are *bad, wrong,* or *should never happen.*

Responding to difference as an attack is one reason why thorny disputes become so deep-rooted. With a Relationship Mindset, you won't lash out at the other person, or seek to win an argument at any cost. And you don't prepare for a resolution discussion as you would for a confrontation. Resolution doesn't stand on who makes the best point, or who delivers the telling blow. It isn't a game to play or a fight to win. How we deal with difference is the test. It's compassion, care and attention that brings you closer to each other, and to a place where you can arrive at reconciliation.

I can almost hear you thinking, *that's all good in theory, but you haven't met the person I'm dealing with!*

I know that when you are just beginning to consider the fracture, you aren't in this frame of mind at all. But the Relationship Mindset is the state from which resolution will be accomplished. Anything else only creates greater distance and antipathy. How do you dial up the care and attention?

Enhance your awareness

Listening and observing attentively **are as important** as the words you exchange during this talk.

I know, I know. Adopt the Mindset. Follow the Protocol. Use the RGS. Now I ask you to bring even more?

These issues are gnarly! But when you incorporate listening skills and body sensibility into your repertoire, I know *you will be ready and equal to the task* when it's time to parley.

Ready for what? The unexpected. Step 5 asks you to open yourself to whatever the other person has to say. Your ego may get jumpy, uneasy at the prospect. What if things head off in directions your ego dislikes? Even though you don't know what's coming, you can prepare for it.

Emotions are already heightened and about to become even more so. You can use your anxiety – not to gird yourself against adversity, but to give yourself a focused task. Convert your nervous energy, and calm your jitters. **Listening** and **observing** both smooth the roadway forward. When you bear down hard with these skills, your mind is so busy picking up insights, it's diverted from nervous worry.

The good news is you don't have to take a special course to improve these skills. Just read on.

Active Listening

When you listen *actively* (as distinguished from passively), you:

- *Pay attention* – give the other person your undivided focus. Steer away from your own distracting activities or thoughts and encourage the other person to speak. Banish your internal chatter – forget about rehearsing what you'll say next, analyzing what's been said, speculating on meaning, stewing in your emotions, or checking your cellphone! Zero in on your counterpart, really listen to their words, and stay in the here and now.

- *Let the silence work* – your counterpart will pause from time to time. Don't rush to comment. Allowing their words to hang in the air can often produce the next big breakthrough.
- *Show you're listening* – mind your own posture and facial expressions. Adjust your body position to show openness and involvement – uncross your arms, lean forward, make eye contact, smooth your brow...
- *Stay calm* – soothe yourself by listening deeply and observing intently. Clear away any immediate judgement of what's being said. Activate your curiosity and just concentrate on the words.
- *Paraphrase what they say* – summarize or, better yet, restate what you just heard them say. Let them correct any misunderstanding.
- *Gather new information* – Mickey Connolly is the founder of Conversant Inc. He says, "The test for listening is learning." If you listen to someone for half an hour and can't say what you learned, you totally wasted that time. Conversations are meant for you to acquire insights you didn't have before. And with them, to move to new places.
- *Ask questions* – find even more clarity by encouraging the other person to reveal greater detail. "Tell me more about...? What else was there...? How did that come about?"

If it all gets to be too much, or if things get really heated or weird, or a potentially damaging track is emerging in the discussion, signal for a time out. Take five, and settle down – both of you! But don't break off. When you're limiting out, use your hands to make the classic 'T' to signal *time out.*

Involvement in this way requires intense focus. It keeps your mind off yourself, shows you're tracking, and helps you *get* the meaning of what's said. It's what every speaker most wants! Active listening is a wonderful life skill. I encourage you to check online resources, videos, and guides to learn more about it.

Body sensibility

Body Language is the unspoken component of communication that lays bare underlying feelings and emotions. The practice of observing the body – facial expressions, arm/leg postures, gestures, tics, fidgets, and the like – lets you in on what others are thinking or feeling beyond and beneath their words. To access such insight, you must expand your awareness to the other person's physical presentation and reactions as you talk together. Do they:

- turn aside
- squirm
- look away
- stare at you
- drop their shoulders
- clench their jaw
- sit back and relax
- inhale sharply
- grin openly
- sigh or exhale slowly?

Are these positive or negative signals? It doesn't take a specialist to intuit signs of distaste, avoidance, interest or welcome. Physical responses are driven by the subconscious and are simply clues to your counterpart's inner reality. You can *see* their edges – the boundaries of what they can or cannot accept – not as they state them, but as they express them with a physicality they can't hide.

Maintaining awareness of how *your own* body presents in this (or any) situation is indispensable too. You can't stage-manage your body's unconscious reactions – that's just you being you! But when you understand how physical signals may open or close the gate of disclosure, you may want to work a bit harder at how you show yourself. With greater awareness, if you happen to catch yourself with, say:

- brows knit
- eyes averted
- hands twitching
- posture suddenly altered…

you can adjust quickly to encourage more flow from the other.

Or, when you notice what's going on within you, you might question what's stirred up? Why you are responding physically in this manner?

You have a wiser perspective available to you known as the *Witness.* Susan Scott calls it your 'personal intelligence agent'. It is a detached viewpoint you can call up. It observes you from above the fray. From its calm place above the storm, it notices your involuntary moves and prompts you to wonder… *What just happened? Were my own boundaries just crossed?*

Knowledge of your body language brings you to terms with the deep sources of your subconsciously triggered behaviors. When I say subconscious, I mean **you can't get at it through normal thought processes.** You have to cue into your body; it tells you there's something going on that you wouldn't otherwise know about.

Boundaries

We are born with extreme levels of sensitivity. Coping with such openness is just too hard in this rough and tumble world. Over time and with repeated bumping, the body builds a tougher, crustier skin of defence. We get hardened off by experience. But a soft membrane remains underneath.

Both you and your VIP have been hurt at that deeper level through the incident – injured and deeply affected by what has happened. You've grown a scarred exterior skin in relation to each other. It closes you off and defends you from further emotional damage. Underneath lies very tender skin which senses what's going on around you on several levels, and absorbs wisdom from the world.

The incident bruised that internal, vulnerable layer... the same one that normally lets you get closer to each other. So, when your conversation touches on or near that bruised place, internal warning bells will go off. Instead of shutting down, take it as a sign that you *should* approach this issue; it truly needs to be worked through.

The body never lies. Even though people create that crusty layer, the body can't neutralize what's happening underneath. Your VIP's body (and yours) will disclose the impact of all that's said or done in the conversation. It is acutely alive and involuntarily expresses when lines are being crossed. If you attune yourself to the signs that the tender layer has been affected, you will be better able to hone in on the core of the issue.

Watch for the boundaries in this interplay between David and Leonora.

> Leonora: [*leaning forward with both arms on the table, eyes flashing*] "I felt this was a definite overreaction."

> David: [*dropping his voice and sitting back a bit*] "Why do you say so?"

> Leonora: [*rising in her chair*] "Because we had it in hand! Or at least we were working on it. You just jumped in and started to put your own plan into action!"

> David: [*responding with curiosity, not argument or justification*] "Tell me more…"

> Leonora: [*settling back a bit, dropping her arms, looking aside*] "Everyone – well, you – assumed nobody was doing anything about the short. Nobody asked me what *we* were doing, or how we were handling it…"

> David: [*restating for clarity*] "So I didn't make any inquiry as to what you'd already done? How were you handling it?"

Leonora: [*eyes softening, tilting forward as she feels heard*] "We had actually done a lot. And right then I had to respond to a call about a substitute shipment that I was trying to arrange. That's why I had to step out. When you started to run on with your own alternatives, you didn't even know we already had things underway to get more flour over here before we ran out…Geez!!" [*sighs and shrugs, looking away*]

David: [*mirroring her emotions*] "You're upset, telling me this…and maybe a bit resigned."

Leonora: "I really am. I felt this meeting was run in a very unfair way. I think we could all have shown cooler heads and not gotten so scrambled up."

David: [*leaning forward*] "So tell me what was happening…"

Leonora: [*breathing out, then brightening*] "Well, that call was to nail down the arrival time for a second truck with half a shipment of flour that afternoon… like I said… before we ran out of supply. After you got going with your plans, I couldn't get a word in edgewise. I could only tell the others later that it was looked after [*fingers tapping on the table*].

David: "I can see you really felt bypassed. And discounted."

Leonora: "Damn right!"

Notice that David does not rise to any provocative comments that Leonora makes; and she is clearly activated. He asks open questions to get more information. And their physical conversation is just as lively as what is being said. David watches Leonora carefully but isn't a detached observer. He cares about her and really wants to get to the bottom of this embarrassing, possibly show-stopping incident. He doesn't deflect her emotions but summarizes and reflects them to her. She needs to sense that he's *getting* her exasperation.

Body language interpretation is an advanced practice! Without deeper training, you will be best served by just stating what you saw, or by allowing your observations to inform the totality of what the other person puts forth.

Making careful comments about another's body language can enhance your exchanges. If your VIP's eyes suddenly gaze off over your shoulder into the distance, you might quietly inquire, "What just happened there?" You may surprise them with this question, and initially make them feel defensive. But it's very likely they will tell you where their thoughts went at that juncture. And that's where you need to go with them.

The warriorship of vulnerability

"No matter what anyone has done to us in the past, or is doing to us now, or might do to us in the future, an innermost, hidden center of ourselves remains invincibly established..."

— JAMES FINLEY

Can you be stronger by opening yourself up?

If another person can taunt you, fluster you by pricking your ego, or by speaking about events or words you'd rather not hear, you remain potentially weak. It's easy for them to poke at you, and push you off your game. And some people can't help themselves... they play at that.

Central to the Protocol is maintaining your poise. If you have a lot to protect by keeping some things secret, those are exactly the places where you can be thrown off. The ego can fire up pretty easily. After all it's kept you stuck by holding onto your rightness to this point. If you can relax about those touchy matters, they lose their power over you.

Opening up and greeting all your own imperfections is at first embarrassing. But if you can face into them honestly, you will experience that they have nothing to do with your core value, or your essence as a human. We are all imperfect. Giving up self-protections lets you stand in that essence. And no one has the power to damage that, unless you let them.

It takes the strength of a warrior to stand open to whatever comes.

Step 5 and beyond

The purpose of the skills outlined in this chapter is to *sensitize* you to what's going on with your VIP, rather than arm you more subtly for conflict. As John Konstanturos used to say,

"We don't teach this to provide you with tools for more enlightened blaming!"

This approach to reaching resolution works precisely because you discard armor and defensiveness, and face the other party *less* equipped for battle. You remain open and alert to your VIP, focused, watching, listening, learning. You let go, freely move with the energy currents of the conversation, and adapt to whatever comes your way.

You can do this!

Now,

- Press on with the Protocol, extend and open yourself, become changed by the rich vitality of the exchange.
- Increase your ability to truly see and hear others, and discover how your viewpoint alters.
- Recognize that difference is natural rather than bad, and adjust your perspective accordingly.

Because of all you're learning and doing, you can more easily stay in sync with each other, remain composed and competent, and able to track together.

It's a tall order but one I hope you see is within your power to orchestrate, conduct and take to conclusion.

Leonora and David have given you a taste of what's just around the next bend on this road. It's a remarkable viewpoint...

Step 5
The view from there

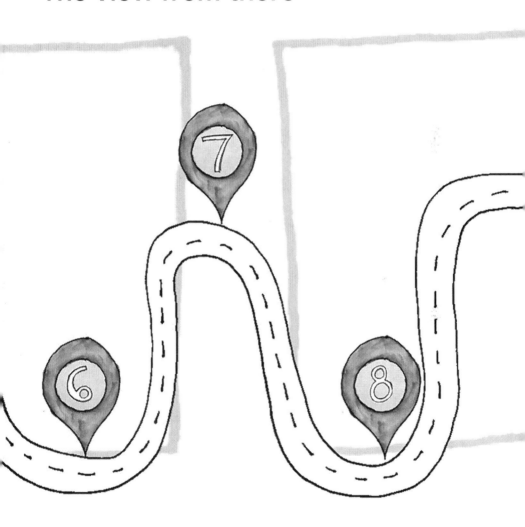

The Resolution Protocol

STEP 1   Describe your role and relationship
          to the other person.

STEP 2   Outline the facts of a single incident
          that led to the relationship break.

STEP 3   Express your emotional reaction to the
          situation and its impact on your identity.

STEP 4   Declare your part in creating or
          continuing the situation.

STEP 5   **Listen to their version of
          what happened, and their
          emotional reaction.**

STEP 6   Describe your expectations of what
          is required to set matters right.

STEP 7   Negotiate a path forward to
          rectify the situation.

STEP 8   Clarify your new agreement, and affirm
          your restored common purpose.

You are stepping up your conversation game, primed with skills, practices and tools that position you as a solid listener. You're going to need all of that to quiet your own busy mind and give your VIP your complete attention now.

This is a long chapter for a good reason. With Step 5 you enter a new phase where you stand back from directing the process and stop talking. It may elevate your nervousness – this is the core of avoidance that has kept you from healing this fracture until now.

Your job in this step is to listen. You elicit and receive a full version of the incident, solely from your VIP's perspective. You hush your '*yeah, but...*' defenses, and set your sights on something much more valuable – the whole story.

Truth origami

John Konstanturos had a wonderful way to illustrate Step 5 to participants in a facilitated resolution session.

He'd hold up a compactly folded bit of paper he'd tightly packed into a tiny square. As he talked about how each version of an incident is one-sided (remember the Beach Ball), he would casually, almost absently, unfold it, a step at a time.

Participants would gradually see more and more in his hands. At the end, he would hold up the fully-opened piece of paper and declare,

"The truth is always unfolding."

The thread of this conversation is leaving your control. You're as ready as you can be to take this step, and enter an honest, unpredictable, and *mutual* conversation. It's only by hearing your VIP's account of the incident that you will ever find enough common ground to work things out.

But you're still guiding the talk, and may intervene occasionally, usually to keep the conversation on topic. The less you do now, the better. Don't let your nervousness spark you to jump in.

It's daunting

Having just gone through Steps 1 to 4, you have some notion of what's to come. But probably not all of it! The other person has learned what happened in the incident from your point of view. Some of it was probably outside their awareness. Perhaps it is already changing what they think and feel about the issue between you. The same is about to happen to you.

It's unknown territory; you have few clues as to what your VIP is about to reveal. If you've set the stage well and they speak freely, there may be a lot for you to take in. And it's possible that what you encounter will impact you, even disturb you. Remember that you've come to this point precisely so you *can* be affected by what you hear, and accordingly, adjust your basis for interacting with them. As Susan Scott says, "If we entertain multiple realities, we create possibilities that did not exist for us before."

Truly, you offer your VIP a very appealing prospect. To someone who has long held onto a complaint or concern – probably because they didn't think you could handle working on it – it's highly satisfying to be able to share their viewpoint. Particularly when it's clear they will be heard. And as you talk together, it begins to dawn on you both that everything you exchange – however rough its form – will contribute to the eventual resolution.

Why does opening yourself up to hear their story cause you anxiety… so much so that you've kept this situation under wraps potentially for years? This is the biggest deal of the entire process – something has kept you from facing this before now:

- Do you have a visceral fear of being overwhelmed by what they say?
- Are you desperately afraid that the emotional blowback will be outsized and you'll be incapable of managing the situation?
- Do you think you won't be able to bear facing up to what they reveal?
- To use a fight paradigm, are you worried you won't be able to block the dagger they might thrust at you in argument?
- Are you embarrassed about your part in the incident, and afraid of being shamed?
- Are you concerned that any attempt to resolve the situation will backfire?

Nobody wants to set themselves up to face a firestorm. But in my experience, what will come won't be as extensive as you imagined. And you are far more resilient than you know. This is all going to be for the better. So just be kind to that scared part of you that wants to duck and run.

How do you cope as the temperature rises?

Rely on the skills described in the previous chapter to focus on what you're hearing and seeing, and avoid fixating on your own reactions.

- Free your mind from preparing defensive retorts to what you hear.
- Still the urge to move quickly through this part of the conversation; to just get it over with.
- Restate and paraphrase what you hear, to be sure you got it right.
- Ask questions to draw out more details.
- Dial up your observations.
- Tame your instinct to fight back and focus instead on what you are learning.

Interrupters

Many people learn or evolve personal coping mechanisms to help them cool down when provoked. Rather than firing back based on raw instinct, they use the Witness and the RGS to inject a higher-level perspective into their thought stream.

In the face of upset, counting internally – 1, 2, 3, 4… – is the simplest mechanism I know.

Mickey Connolly (Conversant Inc.) teaches people in intense circumstances to note the color of the wall. Or pay attention to the furniture. Or repeat a mantra over and over in their minds, like *Caring, caring, caring.*

The aim is to enlist your more evolved brain rather than to let your primitive urges participate in a train wreck.

Whatever tools you have in your mental toolkit to settle yourself down when emotions are storming, be ready to use them now.

All of this is to prepare you for the outsized comeback you fear. It may not happen. The rupture may simply be caused by a misunderstanding of facts that lies beneath the discord – some key element that, had it been known, would have entirely changed how the incident went down.

I'm not saying that your VIP won't come at you hard – there's a possibility. These are delicate but decidedly animated chats! Even amid high emotions, the Relationship Mindset helps you do your utmost to keep the both of you in the room, moving together to the goal.

You are correct if you feel the Protocol flies in the face of popular notions that urge you to *push on, drive hard for what you believe, stick to your guns, show them how it's done...*

Imagine if you tried to assert your opinions, take command, and try to coerce the other party to accept your 'correct' version of events. You'd come across as superior and dismissive. The other person would oppose, then resent your attempt to overwhelm them. They'd become defensive, and strike back with surprising aggression. If you made them fearful, they would become evasive, or maybe submissive. Think how the RGS would flare! The Protocol approach could not work in such an atmosphere.

However, in my experience, the Initiator is always taken aback by what they learn now. They think they have a lock on the situation and perfectly recall everything about it. They soon realize their memory is selective and serves their ego. They learn how differently their VIP experienced and noticed things, and see that some parts of the incident had more dimension or meaning than they knew. They perceive how fiercely or mildly their VIP felt.

Ready, set, go

If you have successfully framed the discussion, the other party will be frank with you now, despite that they are likely as bruised and tender over the situation as you. If they lash out, hear them through, then bring them back.

Emotion demonstrates significance. It reveals an exposed nerve, something central you need to know. Is it worth enduring an outburst, so you can understand what happened to cause the break between you? If you're determined to get to the bottom of the breach, I think so.

Kick off Step 5 with a simple, open-ended question that encourages your VIP to speak their part, for example:

I'd like to know what happened from your perspective.

Would you please tell me fully what went on?

Can I hear what transpired?

How do you see things?

What's happened in this for you?

If your VIP feels safe, and the ground is clear of bias and agenda, they will respond. Your mission then is to keep them talking (and yourself listening). Pretend you know nothing. Ask as many questions as necessary to obtain a complete and rich version of the situation – facts and emotions.

Use open-ended queries rather than those that can be answered with a *Yes* or *No*. Avoid leading questions, ones that suggest the answer. Stay away from anything that has to do with *why*. You want facts not speculation. Here are some sample open-ended questions:

> *What was the worst/best part of…?*
> *What is it that you like/dislike…?*
> *How did that affect you?*
> *How would you do it differently?*
> *What caused that?*
> *How would things have changed if…?*
> *What was going on when…?*
> *What happened that time…?*
> *How did that come about?*
> *What makes you say…?*
> *What did you say/do next?*
> *How did that work…?*

Use them liberally to keep the detail flowing about places, people, feelings, things, what was said, done or produced… Recall the topics you yourself covered in Steps 1 to 4:

- Their view of roles and this relationship, and ways you two interact
- What happened for them in this precise incident
- How they felt or were impacted by what happened
- Offerings of responsibility

Be crisp, clean, and clear with your inquiries. Longer questions are almost always attempted manipulations on your part. Simple questions asked with good intent always draw out the most information! If, on the other hand, you use questions to validate what you think you know, confirmation bias will keep you rooted unhelpfully in your version.

Here's how David gets Leonora talking in Step 5:

"Please tell me now how this all unfolded for you."

"Well, I came to the meeting fairly well prepared, I thought." [A little defensiveness and a one-shot answer are not uncommon at this point.]

"What did you have ready?"

"I had built a spreadsheet showing our upstream supply chain status and was ready to go through it."

"I didn't know that."

"We never got to it. You got so alarmed hearing from Production about low supplies, we were in damage control right away. But I already knew where the problem was…"

"What had you found out?"

"Just before I came into the meeting, I heard that the Atlas truck containing our delivery had crashed on the I-30 the day before. I knew it wouldn't be coming, and we were stuck."

"What else did you learn?"

"The day before that…"

Notice how David stays in his lane, and asks question after question. Alternately, David could have worked with Leonora to construct a timeline of events. He might have obtained even more information that way.

What if it seems to be going wrong?

When you turn the floor over to your VIP, expect them to respond. Their initial reaction may be a defensive move. They could:

- Cave, and fall all over themselves trying to instantly fix you [Appease]
- Turn aside, refuse to make eye contact, and clam up [Freeze]
- Look for the exits, and make excuses to leave the room [Flee]
- Go on the offensive and strike out at you [Fight]

While any of these responses will fire your RGS and may slow the progress of the discussion, they may simply *need* to be expressed. After all, you both created the fracture, and you must both explore its circumstances each using your own words given in your own unique styles.

If you face defensive reactions, meet them with compassion. Look beyond the emotional surge. The Relationship Mindset makes space for you both. Hold fast to your sense of care and concern for your VIP and let the conversation go where it must.

You'll be fine. You have nothing else to do but listen actively, observe carefully, and stow any unproductive opposition lurking in your depths.

> ⚠️ *Please... don't hand them this book as a means to get them to perform their part right!*

Rely on the RGS to steer away from dark emotions, use interrupters (your mantra) to keep your cool, and respond carefully to provocation or negative remarks. It will take all your composure to stay on course, to avoid slipping away from the RGS centerline that points to your destination.

If, however your VIP seems mired in a reactive, defensive mode, it's probably because you didn't go far enough with Step 4. You didn't convince them that you are 100% accountable for causing and sustaining the situation, and that 0% of the responsibility is theirs.

Calling a Temporary Halt

Or, maybe they're just not ready. This is a lot to contend with; it could be a temporary showstopper. Maybe they already wrestled with the effects of the situation and it no longer acutely troubles them. Or perhaps they are pretending that's the case, so they can hold onto their self-esteem. To suddenly rip that bandage off is intimidating. They may be incapable of continuing in the moment.

If they can't or won't share their side of the story, it's okay. You can resume this conversation another time, if it falters now. Sometimes people just need to pause; to back off, to process what they heard, to digest. This doesn't mean your initiative has failed. It simply needs some time to take hold. Not  everyone can respond easily on the fly. Personalities are different, and people have varying capacities for this sort of thing. So, taking a short time out – nothing more – can allow them to gather themselves.

Really? I lead you all this way, and tell you to just stop if it doesn't go well? Remember, the Relationship Mindset underpins the Protocol. It wants two competent people to be able to venture into a highly charged situation, remaining whole and self-controlled throughout.

Some of you may feel that this has been a lengthy meeting already, without any appropriate breaks. It isn't generally a good idea to interrupt the Flow. Even though you're jumpy, it probably hasn't really been all that long. This is a nervous reaction. I can't say how long it should take for you to get to this point. But my experience is that the anxiety in the air makes both of you feel antsy and looking for any opening to break it off. Best you don't, unless matters have really come to a wall, or one of you acutely needs to gather yourself. Keep going. It's difficult to recover if you break the momentum of constructive progress.

A short pause may be politic but my experience is that breaking this meeting into multiple sessions reduces the drive to get to the core of the fracture.

However, if things have come to a very tough pass and there seems no way through, you can consider adjourning for a bit...

> *Maybe let's take a break.*
>
> *How about we get together again in a couple of hours?*
>
> *Can we please set a time now so it doesn't go by the wayside?*

You may be surprised that just letting the pressure off for a moment is enough to break open the logjam right then. The mere suggestion of a break is enough, and the meaty talk gets rolling.

No method or device can resolve this temporary blockage. The incident lays before the two of you like a surgically opened body on an operating table. Let **space and silence** do what words cannot.

If one of the parties is temporarily unhinged, it's better to halt the process. It's foolish to bull on when someone is enraged, has gone completely silent, or is distraught and cannot be calmed. To continue may well re-wound your VIP, and send them back behind their walls.

Are you disappointed that I don't have a magic wand for you to overcome this sort of energy? In my practice, I've seen many people work through heavy emotional displays, but I can't claim this approach tames every tiger. No technique can do that. But I can tell you that a break in the conversation happens only very rarely. Potentially encountering that risk should certainly not prevent you from embarking on this journey with the Protocol.

Generally, these are good people, not ogres. Most often they know something is wrong and have been bothered by it too. They are also reluctantly aware they've had a hand in causing it, and want to make it right. So, it's up to you to avoid jumping to conclusions – including that it's impossible to carry on.

Prepare to listen well, and learn

To get ready for your actual talk, review the prior chapter and note a few reminders on your Preparation Worksheet, to have as a ready reference.

Capture your preferred Interrupter tactic, so you can pull it up in a necessary moment. It and the RGS will remind you to avoid primitive reactions.

Be ready for Step 5 to take some time! Generally, it should take your VIP just as long to relay their version, as you took to lay out your story in Steps 1-4. Write out several potential open-ended questions that can help you chase details, get deeper explanations, and be a hedge if your VIP should stop talking too soon.

That said, you want to discourage them from expanding their narrative to other incidents, if you can. They might go there anyway. Gently guide them back to the issue at hand.

> *I'd like to stay with this one situation, if we can. I promise to make time to get into that item with you later.*

You may wonder how you both allow a conversation to unfold as it must, and yet maintain its focus. It's the Relationship Mindset at work again. You reveal your core, caring motivation by your openness, curiosity, humility. Your VIP senses your intention to rise beyond pettiness, and pursue truth. Human nature makes them want to reciprocate. They feel motivated to progress together with you to the objective you set out to achieve.

It isn't easy to be the responsible one, to guide the Flow as you move through this Protocol and master your emotions all at the same time. You must maintain great awareness of what is happening between you both during this discussion, and not allow your jumpiness to start forcing it. The RGS helps you be more aware of the swirling emotions, lets you listen to your Witness in the midst of it all, then take steps that keep you both balanced, centered and on course.

You may be astounded by what you hear. You may experience a sense of release from what has been a long period of recrimination and doubt. Grasping your VIP's dilemma, you learn things you couldn't have anticipated. You acquire much more of the story

⚠️ *You will feel a lot in Step 5. You may not like the sensation of being knocked off your pins. Your ego's ability to stabilize you has been exceeded. Expect to want to self-justify as you listen.*

and it alters your understanding of how and why this situation came about. The experience is often amazing, even cathartic.

That's why you are going to all this trouble.

And that's why I asked you to spend time with this chapter.

Reflect for a moment

The conclusion of Step 5 is very special. Make the most of it!

- Relinquish any sense that you should have seen it all, or known more. You couldn't have.
- Commit to use everything you learned and gained, to craft what's coming next.
- Celebrate that you are not lost, submerged by it all... that you kept your head and your heart.
- Appreciate that you led this conversation, then gave up control to have a responsive dialogue with your VIP.

Your responsibility for the Flow isn't over yet. This viewpoint on the road to resolution has surely changed your perspective. The benefits of your good work will become even more evident as you proceed.

Now it's time to get back in the car, check your bearings, and be reminded of the magnetic place you're headed.

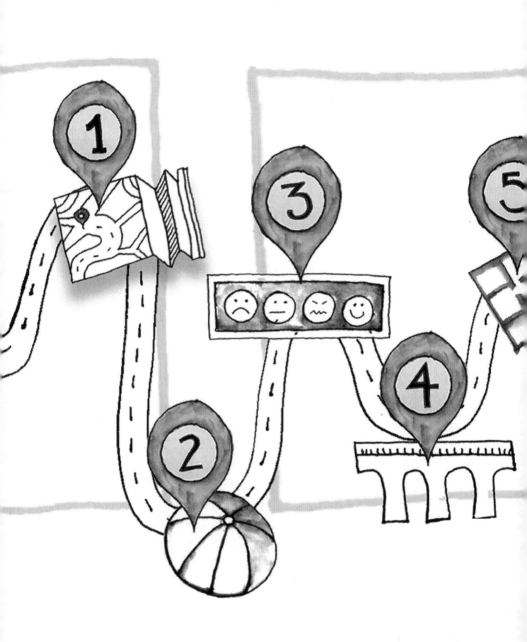

Step 6

Recenter on your destination; recalculating...

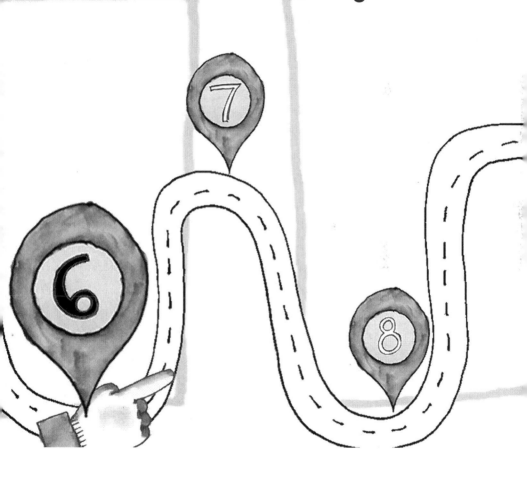

The Resolution Protocol

STEP 1 Describe your role and relationship
to the other person.

STEP 2 Outline the facts of a single incident
that led to the relationship break.

STEP 3 Express your emotional reaction to the
situation and its impact on your identity.

STEP 4 Declare your part in creating or
continuing the situation.

STEP 5 Listen to *their* version of what happened,
and *their* emotional reaction.

STEP 6 **Describe your expectations of what
is required to set matters right.**
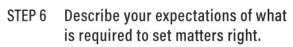

STEP 7 Negotiate a path forward to
rectify the situation.

STEP 8 Clarify your new agreement, and affirm
your restored common purpose.

"The menu is not the meal."

- ALAN WATTS

Your VIP's rich description of the incident has given you more context and a better understanding of the overall situation. Next? Aim the emergent understanding clearly back toward your destination – your desired outcome.

For a while we've explored how the actual conversation will play out.

In Step 6, you take the lead again for a time, putting forward what you think is necessary to settle this issue and [re]build your relationship going forward. It can feel strange. After such deep exploration of each other's circumstances, you may feel done, drained, and tempted to let the whole thing slide into something less purposeful and more comfortable.

In fact, the pull away from discipline can haunt you the whole way through.

> *Why don't I just scrap all this hard stuff and bang the rest of it out?*

> Or... *Let's just knock off and go for beers.*

But you'd fall short of the mark, never reaching that special place you're aiming for.

You've taken pains to come this far. So let your VIP know where this is all going. Return to your Preparation Worksheet, and scribe a statement guided by considerations in this chapter.

The topic? What needs to be different in the next phase of your relationship.

The details you now disclose about what you want to achieve become the template for what you get at the end of this process.

When you're drafting that statement on your Worksheet, you won't have the benefit of the insights you'll acquire during the actual conversation. Before focusing on Pre-Work, let's dwell a moment on the state of the actual discussion.

Press on

You've been listening well and hard to your VIP for a while. So, when exactly do you move on to Step 6?

Listen for signs that your VIP is faltering: they repeat themselves, start to pile up similar facts, have no further details to share, or just naturally run out of gas and heave a deep sigh. They may turn to you and say, "So?"

Your move to resume leadership may be a bit awkward. You got (and kept) them talking, and now you stop the Flow and nudge it toward the negotiation that comes after this.

Bridging statements like these will help you switch gears to take up the reins once more:

> *Whoo!! That's a lot to take in! Now I'd like to...*

> *Thanks so much for telling me. I'm still thinking about what you said, but I want to make sure I say this...*

You've really helped me see how this came about. And I want to talk, just for a moment, about where we can go from here…

Now, get specific about what a suitable outcome would look like for you.

Don't worry about having to be bound completely to this statement. You'll have an opportunity to alter your view in Step 7.

State what you want

It can be tough to clearly lay out the characteristics of your renewed relationship, so (surprise!) it's best to prepare beforehand. It's your final bit of Pre-Work ahead of the conversation.

This step is part of the preparation package you make before the talking ever begins. Bring up the work you did for Steps 1 and 4. Ponder these questions to characterize the new understanding expected between the two of you:

- What can I borrow from my Step 1 role statement preparation? What were the optimal roles and relationship I had in mind then?
- In Step 4, I used 100%→0% analysis to arrive at *woulda / coulda / shoulda* insights that might have changed how matters turned out. How can I capitalize on those now?
- How can I bring the outcome closer to the ideal I compared myself to in Step 4?

The answers are the basis of the declaration you will make, Write it out on your Worksheet. A satisfactory outcome statement usually:

- Is multidimensional; includes emotional and spiritual aspects, not just mechanics
- Is based on your Step 1 and 4 Pre-Work
- Will be adaptable to what you hear in the conversation; makes the most of what you've learned
- Refers to the breach of trust in the incident, to head off a repeat
- Incorporates the foundations that enabled you to interact well together in the past

The atmosphere when you're actually talking will still be sensitive and emotional, so ground whatever you are going to say in the Relationship Mindset. Choose your words carefully, and seek a balance – where you stick to your intentions without alienating your VIP. It's what we strive to do in our daily lives… stay true to self without losing connection to those we care about. It's yet another good reason to write out what you'll say on your Worksheet beforehand.

You don't have to make it a grand statement, but do get clearly to the point. For example:

> *I'd like to bring you back to what I'm looking for out of this talk. I want nothing less than to have the two of us back on a strong foundation, better than before. Here's what I think would work for me…*

When you do arrive at Step 6 in real life, it will be with a much better understanding of your VIP's perspective. So, it's quite possible you'll want to modify this draft statement on the fly. You will have more options, know what to avoid, and what might work better than you ever imagined.

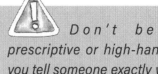 *Don't be too prescriptive or high-handed. If you tell someone exactly what to do or how to be, they'll chafe at the restriction.*

Nevertheless, you must still prepare what you'll say in advance. It will be a solid base that you can easily modify based on what you've what you've heard.

Here's David:

> "Leonora, I'm very glad to have heard from you how this situation developed. And I first want to say this: we can't ever get so close to the line in our supply inventory levels again.
>
> Assuring adequate supply to Production is what you're all about, and I can't tolerate this level of risk. Pulling rabbits out of your hat at the last moment is a style that doesn't work for me. I don't want the drama.
>
> I want us to be stocked up and equipped to produce. That's my job. And I am ready and willing to trust you to be forthright with me as issues arise, but I want to see more anticipation from you.

I'm also determined that you and I work this out to complete satisfaction just between us. I don't view this as something we need to involve others in. I do see it as an opening to a much stronger working relationship between us – personally and in our divisions.

I don't plan on talking about it with anyone else. That includes Alicia. I'd like you to leave Ray out of it too. Depending on what we work out, we may involve our respective senior people.

Now, how are we going to get this right?"

Will your statement be like David's or have a different style? He may seem prescriptive, but his feelings are evident beneath his words: *I trust you. I respect you. I see that you are competent and I want to work with you.* He lays out what he needs, but the underpinning sentiments are implicit. He could have gone even further in verbalizing his feelings of confidence in Leonora...

Ready and able

At this point you're well into the process, have talked together for a while, and grown more confident in your ability to manage the conversation. You've maintained a Relationship Mindset, and kept the Resolution Guidance System at the ready. You're observant, alert, and able to choose your words and actions with care. More and more, you have the hang of this!

Are you surprised by your growing ability to observe yourself in action and direct yourself in the heat of fire? You can thank your inner Witness for keeping an eye on your ego, and for serving up enlightened comments from its detached viewpoint. You've prepared, stuck with it, and can capably choose your responses.

It's my experience that this capacity will only grow the more you practice the Protocol. In the same way I've seen so many others master themselves and rise above these conflicts, you are coming to realize you are more than this situation, or this conversation.

So, trust the Witness again to guide how you prepare and communicate your desired result. Avoid the temptation to describe simple structural or process changes – more collaboration, regular touch-points, shared goals you both can work toward, etc. You might be most comfortable in this territory, but this process is meant to stretch you. The real basis of resolution lies beyond, **within the emotional and spiritual dimensions** of your relationship.

Let yourself reach past the obvious and express your fondest wishes. Say the things that are secretly whispering in your mind. Be bold and fully forthright; ask for what you want and need.

It's almost certain that the outcome you eventually reach will vary somewhat from this declaration you make in Step 6, since, as John Konstanturos used say, quoting Alan Watts:

"The menu is not the meal."

A word of advice... it may be best to try out the process on something less than a blockbuster disagreement your first time out. Find an issue or incident that lets you ride 'with training wheels on' before tackling a more loaded problem.

So now that you've read the menu and tasted the appetizers, it's time to order up the main course! What will make this a satisfying feast?

Your VIP is about to get *their* chance to weigh in on what an ideal relationship between you two should be going forward. In the next step – Negotiation – you'll work jointly to explore and develop solutions that work for both of you. You'll even test them to make sure your choices will hold up.

Your roadmap to resolution points to an exciting stretch of country to cover. So, go on! This is the juicy part... and it's worth the squeeze, I promise!

Step 7

Negotiation; onward with your adventure

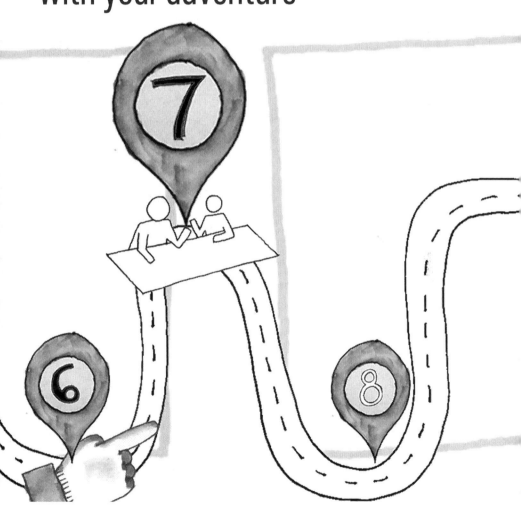

The Resolution Protocol

STEP 1   Describe your role and relationship
          to the other person.

STEP 2   Outline the facts of a single incident
          that led to the relationship break.

STEP 3   Express your emotional reaction to the
          situation and its impact on your identity.

STEP 4   Declare your part in creating or
          continuing the situation.

STEP 5   Listen to *their* version of what happened,
          and *their* emotional reaction.

STEP 6   Describe your expectations of what
          is required to set matters right.

STEP 7   **Negotiate a path forward to
          rectify the situation.**

STEP 8   Clarify your new agreement, and affirm
          your restored common purpose.

*"Out beyond ideas of right-doing
and wrong-doing, there is a
field. I'll meet you there..."*

- RUMI

You and your VIP have built a strong base from which to pursue a better relationship with each other in future. Because of your efforts, the two of you together have come to understand what caused your fracture. You have both persevered through tough emotional territory, and you have just disclosed the destination you have in mind for this resolution passage.

You're still leading this discussion. Here at Step 7, you jointly propose, develop, and come to agreement on the way forward. There is an open road to explore and work together as a team, taking real steps toward making the situation right.

We'll spend at bit of time here at this important juncture. So best to get comfortable in your seat for a bit, while I share this information.

You might have misgivings about negotiating. Perhaps you despair that there is only one way for this to be settled, and doubt your VIP will ever go for it. Maybe you don't believe there is *any* solution that can truly resolve the situation for good, restore your relationship, and go the distance.

You may be discounting your mutual creative powers! The avenues will open. The Resolution Protocol helps you go the extra mile to build more sensitivity and resilience into proposed outcomes.

Get started

Negotiation is a common practice. Most everyone knows the process: identify some options, expand on ideas that seem promising, test the best ones for feasibility, then together determine the ideal blend to put into practice. Crafting a solution to mend your fracture follows this basic approach.

As you begin talking at Step 7, the emotional temperature has likely dropped a bit so the lead-in is simple and natural:

What can we do about this?

I'd like to suggest we try...

What do you think would work...?

How might we...?

Then, open the door to creativity.

Negotiation starts with brainstorming. You want to draw out as many options as the two of you can concoct. No questions or clarifications; just additions. Make a list of them all – good, bad, or crazy. Keep an open mind – don't dismiss ideas that seem odd or risky.

Don't get too formal. It's more important to actually complete the work of Step 7 than to bind yourself to rules and processes.

Also, don't chase any *one* promising idea to exclusion of all others. The value of brainstorming is that the solution you seek lies amid *all* the options you both can dream up. And some you might not have thought of are going to be offered in a minute.

When you focus on what's wrong with ideas, it kills imagination, and prevents other useful options from emerging at all. Stop this tendency as soon as it starts:

⚠ *Do not be drawn into what I call sucker's tennis. By this I mean the remorseless pummeling of the first option surfaced.*

Under withering criticism, early options and ideas can hit the trash before having any real chance. It goes like this... a possibility is ventured, doubts are voiced, value is debated, and the idea gets batted back and forth until it's critiqued to death.

Wait a minute! Before we dig deeper into this idea, I'd like us to get them all on the table.

I've got some more suggestions and I bet you have others too. Let's write them all down so we don't forget any.

What else comes to mind...?

Once you've got an ample list of ideas, your task together is to take a first pass at rating and ranking them. Without big debates, create a short list of the best elements – they don't all have to be complete answers. You may gravitate quickly to the likeliest solutions. Make sure to include the Magic 5 – more on those coming up.

⚠ *Beware the flight into health. In therapy, analysts are ever watchful for the appearance of convenient, immediate 'outs' – easy, quick answers that apparently solve the whole problem and make it go away. This is just avoiding the psychological pressure that must be endured to get to a deeper, lasting solution.*

Decide which ideas, pieces of ideas, suggestions, or combinations contain the seeds of potential resolution. Then when you've found a promising track, get into the nuts and bolts to build out the options into a fully-fledged solution.

Go for meaning

In my experience, some of the most potent options – ideas that make for quantum leaps – don't come to mind so readily. People tend to gravitate to more superficial changes... different roles, placating gifts, a change of scenery, getting other people involved. Not all of these are trivial, and could certainly be components of a proposed resolution agreement. Trouble is, these are generally backdrop changes that don't get at the core problem; the poor dynamics that led to the fracture remain. Sooner or later, the issues could reappear.

Far more rewarding results come when you go deeper and search for meaningful changes that get at the heaviest differences between you. Seek solutions that address the real pain of the fracture. Feelings were hurt and expectations were crushed. Why?

In most long-standing disputes, the cuts go deeper, beyond faulty structural arrangements or even emotional cost. Think about respect. Look to *identities. They* were challenged or disputed; cherished roles called into doubt, competencies questioned, prized reputations tarnished.

> *I'm a professional architect; I was treated like a junior draftsman*
>
> *I know in my heart I'm a really good mother and wife, but...*

I believed myself to be a strong partner, thoughtful and concerned about the welfare of...

Recall that broken trust bucket? And the emphasis I placed on the breach of trust that precipitated this entire discussion? By now both of you *get* the impacts of those breaches. Many were identity shocks.

How does it truly feel when trust breaks? It's not abstract; it scars deep. When character is demeaned, the wounds to self-esteem are profound, and the emotional impacts are intense. There has been intolerable friction between the two parties.

How do you build a solution that salvages such a mess? Here are some tried and true approaches.

The Magic Five

The Magic Five are a set of time-honored methods to repair conflict that the ego shies away from. They have long helped people remedy emotional and spiritual damage.

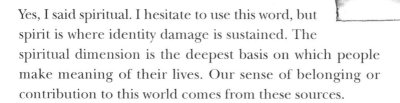

Yes, I said spiritual. I hesitate to use this word, but spirit is where identity damage is sustained. The spiritual dimension is the deepest basis on which people make meaning of their lives. Our sense of belonging or contribution to this world comes from these sources.

Imagine a participant's identity has been impugned – as a parent, a partner, a competent professional. They have been insulted. Their deepest expectations, their most profound attachments to people, their sense of how they add value to workplace, family and community, and their ideals have been dashed. These wounds occurred in the spiritual dimension, and the resolution discussion must repair them at that level. That doesn't mean other manifestations or behaviors might not need to shift.

The Magic Five are exactly the vital, old-school devices that help shape a profound, negotiated solution.

- **Apologies** – who needs to hear 'sorry', and for what behavior, specifically?
- **Acknowledgements** – what damage has been done or contributions made that must be explicitly identified and spoken out in the open?
- **Undertakings** – what action was taken that requires assurance it will never be committed again? What requisite must always be done in future? And how can these be given and believed?
- **Amends** – what can be done now, as compensation in the present, to make this right?
- **Forgiveness** – what can be released, given up, never to be raised again?

You can read more about the Magic Five at *DougBouey.com/ ffdownloads.*

The best solutions include more than just a dash of the Magic Five – they are central.

To mend the break, offer your VIP an appropriate mix of practicalities and the Magic Five elements with full, unreserved sincerity.

Your ego, of course, won't want anything to do with this. The Magic Five reveal your essential vulnerability. They ask you to open yourself up, take radical ownership of your $100\% \rightarrow 0\%$ inventory, make admissions, and seek rectification without conditions. In this, you will draw from the well of your courage to rise above your smaller self.

There is no secret recipe, and no way to know how much of each element you need, how to order them, when you've said too much, or not enough. Once you know they have a place at the table, they emerge almost involuntarily during the discussion. They can happen anytime.

I can only say that you must look inside yourself, to your soul, and ask:

What do I most dread saying?

What does my VIP really need and want to hear?

What are they deeply asking for?

What will reveal my true self, warts and all, if say it?

John K always said,

"Ante up first."

And so, you (as Initiator) begin. You supplied your first dose of the Magic Five when you took $100\% \rightarrow 0\%$ accountability. It was one long Acknowledgement! More can come forward now. Open by saying, *I was wrong.* Take a deep breath, step around your pride, and start talking.

Don't be surprised if your VIP reciprocates! Was this entirely your creation? Probably not, but until the defences go down, more constructive joint accountability is not possible.

This isn't trading. You don't tender a token, then wait for long-sought admissions from the other. Be unreserved; tap into it all. Your investment in coming forward first will be borne out by your VIP's wholehearted response.

Sometimes Magic Five statements are a bit awkward and incomplete. But they still work!

Here, David gives it a try first, then Leonora chimes in:

> "I'm sorry that I didn't act as a better peer should have, when you wandered into this risky territory and I didn't speak to you about it.
>
> I've also stood by while my team has complained about your division. I haven't stopped that, and I didn't get out in front of the issue by pulling our two groups together."

> "Dave, I am truly sorry about taking you and the company to the brink like that. You're right. There is a part of me that can be cavalier about risk. That might be okay in my personal life, but it sure isn't okay for Dugmore Foods. I recognize the peril I placed you and this company in.
>
> I just hope we can move beyond this… not to forget it, but to be careful about it in future. I'm certainly going to watch very closely whenever I sense I might be getting a bit of a thrill by taking things too close to the line. And

if you notice it happening, I'd appreciate it if you would bring it to my attention, if I seem to be unaware of it."

David's Apology is straightforward. Leonora's Magic Five mix is more full, and includes an Apology, an Acknowledgement, and an Undertaking.

Endurance testing

Suppose you have crafted a provisional solution together. You have each expressed some Magic Five elements, are ready to make a few adjustments, and have found a workable way to bring your difficult situation back on track. How do you know your proposal will stand up over time? It would be a terrible shame to go through all this and find yourself back at square one a few weeks from now.

You and your VIP have history... other incidents, not-great interactions, unpleasant situations where you disappointed each other. These old patterns can resurface and put new agreements at risk. That possibility must be prevented.

To ensure your joint proposal lasts, you must check for leaks in your trust bucket. For each provisional solution you create, you must ask aloud:

"What might sabotage this resolution?"

When you ask and both of you answer this question, you've begun to bullet-proof your resolution.

How does this work?

First you can expect to resist asking the question. Both of you are naturally relieved to finally be pursuing options that will put your relationship back together. You don't want anything to jeopardize this delicate new working arrangement.

But asking *what might sabotage your resolution* is **the essential extra step** that John Konstanturos added to the basic Negotiation process. It distinguishes the Resolution Protocol. Answering this question – as many times as necessary – secures true completion, such that the fracture never occurs again.

What if...?

I can't go any further without addressing a question that may be surging up from your doubting mind at this point!

If you've laid strong groundwork, you are probably seeing distinct signs of a thaw right now. It's a discussion – you're talking back and forth. If you are making good progress and are supportive of each other, it's a good indication of great things to come.

But you may still be facing some show-stopper moments. Your VIP may come up with something that really throws you. Or they stonewall... arms folded, looking down or staring fixedly at you. What now?

If you're working too hard and not getting much back, it's time to pause. Body language will likely have been signalling for a halt for some time. Some mirroring may help:

> *Your arms are folded and you haven't said anything for a while...*

Then make a naked admission of failure!

Let's stop. What am I doing wrong here? What have I missed? You aren't offering anything to help us move forward...

I've seen how a return to purpose can ground the Initiator when things go off kilter. It's that silent mantra, *Caring, caring, caring,* that brings the higher brain to the party.

Repeat it inside and slow down the play. Don't mind the silence; it works on them too. Susan Scott says silence is 'where what is real can be detected'. Just don't turn this into a standoff, or a stare-down to see who blinks first.

Say something once you've regained your ground. Usually, the hang up is back up the road in an earlier component of the discussion. Retrace your steps and proceed again more carefully, while soliciting more feedback and clarification on earlier points. Go back and improvise. You'll be surprised by what can come up, now that you're this far along...

Rinse and repeat

You've been dealing with this single incident. With the '**what might...**' question, you will fire up memories of previous unresolved issues. These past breaches of trust must also be surfaced and worked through. It's now that your good work to bring both of you safely to this point really starts to pay off.

Prompted by the answers to '**what might sabotage**...', the two of you need to cycle back and delve into each past doubtful incident. Each disappointment between you, each loss of trust must be brought up in sequence, and explored *one by one*, in the same careful Protocol way.

You might be reluctant. You took extravagant care to ensure both of you remained capable, confident and in full possession of yourselves. And you haven't created undue emotional trauma. It's a real tribute to your attentiveness and your ability to focus on that one incident. But you're not so delicate that you can't go the whole distance. Your good work set the stage to deploy the durability test. Seize the opportunity in the open channel of communication between you now. It's fertile ground to sow, and later to harvest your rewards.

You do all of this on the fly, without the thoughtful preparation you did for the one incident that centered this conversation. Yes, you might blunder a bit or choose some less than appropriate words as you improvise. Take as much care as the setting will allow, but go forward now, while you are both still sensitized. Your VIP will cut you some slack. Pause briefly as necessary, to recall together anything else that arises when you ask,

"What might sabotage this resolution?"

Here's David, bravely venturing into the unknown…

"Leonora, your openness is really helping us resolve this problem between us. What might sabotage our idea to advance the timing of Production readiness meetings?

Three months ago, we encountered a similar issue on packaging. I proposed that we stockpile

Coconut Cruise boxes to avoid stockouts. Do you recall that discussion?

We didn't end up doing that, and later it created a problem. I think we need to talk through that situation to make our reliance on each other stronger..."

Drive to capture every issue that needs attention. Each has in some way contributed to your broken relationship. This is your worthy adventure... explore each one fully in a careful, considerate way. Don't lose momentum by breaking off for a nap by the roadway. You're cooking now! Usually, each item can be dispatched with the ease that comes in a far less defensive conversation.

Both of you have expanded your capability for resolution, but it's new. Strong discipline is still necessary. It's too easy to throw over all the good learning you've acquired and revert to an unschooled attack regarding one or more of these additional incidents. Watch your RGS and be quick to say *whoa!* if this happens. Hold yourself in check and be the Chair. Maintain the Relationship Mindset, consult the *Protocol on a Page* (from the Appendix, or *DougBouey.com/ ffdownloads*) and run the Flow as needed to deal in the same careful way with each of the incidents in turn.

It may take a while – maybe as long as another hour – to process the other situations that prevent you from fully trusting each other. Expect some heart-rending moments, more emotions, and some surprises – not all pleasant. This continuation is completely worth the effort. Go for the whole enchilada! Add whatever comes out of this stress-testing to your provisional resolution. Your new trust bucket will be stronger and even more full after these collateral issues are explored and tested.

While the basic framework for negotiation is familiar to most, in this Chapter I've superimposed elements that are uniquely appropriate to reaching a solution to a painfully fractured relationship. Together they take you to the required depth to truly accomplish what you set out to do.

 As Step 7 concludes, you have in hand a proposal for resolution that's reinforced against failure, and a newly mended trust bucket. You have tempered the spiritual damage caused by this break, with honest and complete assertions and commitments. The gold of your repairs shines bright!

You are about to achieve what others thought impossible. Resolution.

Step 8

Arrive in style; confirmation and commitment

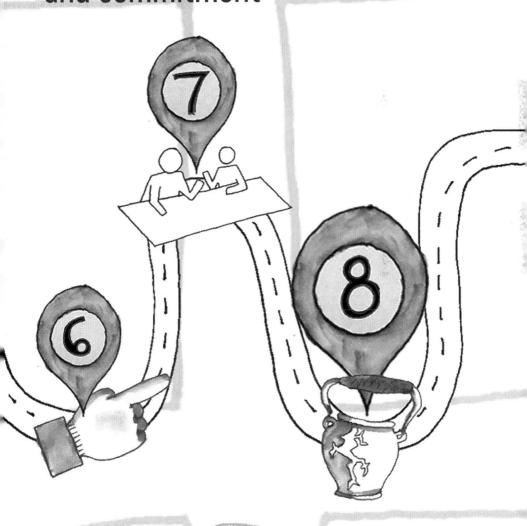

The Resolution Protocol

STEP 1   Describe your role and relationship to the other person.

STEP 2   Outline the facts of a single incident that led to the relationship break.

STEP 3   Express your emotional reaction to the situation and its impact on your identity.

STEP 4   Declare your part in creating or continuing the situation.

STEP 5   Listen to *their* version of what happened, and *their* emotional reaction.

STEP 6   Describe your expectations of what is required to set matters right.

STEP 7   Negotiate a path forward to rectify the situation.

STEP 8   **Clarify your new agreement, and affirm your restored common purpose.**

"You know you're on the
right track when you become
uninterested in looking back."

- UNKNOWN

You've gone the distance, done the heavy lifting with the Protocol. You've arrived at a resolution agreement, perhaps hard won. You have a feeling of relief and a glow of satisfaction. Your VIP looks at you with – could it be? – renewed regard, even fondness?

Don't skip this

The finish line is in sight. This is the final step of the Protocol. You might feel out of gas, tempted to stand up, stretch your legs, and signal a break-off. So great is your elation at finally working through the gnarly threads of your differences, you may wish to omit Step 8. Don't. No resolution is complete without it.

Do it all. Do it well.

Resume leadership of the Flow one last time. This step adds grace to your resolution, and your VIP might not sense the importance of closing with strength that Step 8 brings.

It's time to wind up this conversation with class and style. You fashioned your proposal amid strong emotions, and as a result the particulars may be difficult to recall later. Two final actions are therefore necessary to confidently close out your encounter.

1. **Create a clear and accurate summary of what has been settled between you.**

   Document your outcome while it is still fresh in both your minds. When you restate all the components of your new agreement, you consolidate and cement your changed circumstances. You make clear specifically what you can expect from each other.

   Use the space provided on your Preparation Worksheet to write out the details of your resolution agreement. Clarity is important. Apologies have been accepted, undertakings have been given for the future, people need to be spoken with, arrangements must be made. None of these are unimportant or trivial; they are responses to issues you discussed, and repaired.

   As you recap your deal and note down the details, you may find surprising omissions or holes in your agreement. So, while the conciliatory mood is with you, take time to fill in the gaps. You'll be glad you did. No one knows better than you what it takes to create this special atmosphere.

2. **Declare a renewed and strengthened relationship going forward.**

   The final component of your agreement ought to express appreciation for the fine association the two of you have, and how this work has reaffirmed it. It should be stated outright that you have strengthened, reshaped, and deepened your relationship, and have a new foundation. Don't assume that it's implied by other aspects of your agreement. Reliance on assumptions is part of what divided you to begin with.

Communiqué

Others may be inescapably involved in your relationship. Friends, co-workers, relatives, and others all around you have quietly endured the impacts of your broken trust. They've danced around the distance you've built between you, endured stony silences, biased interpretations, and crabbed interactions. They've walked on eggshells and had to create workarounds. With the clarity of resolution, you can each see the costs imposed on them by your trust breaches.

These people have long hoped for something like this resolution conversation to occur. They deserve to know that the issues between you have been resolved, and how your agreement may affect them. Let these folks in on how things have changed; it releases the pressure on them. Even if you feel they will just *know*, it's best to be upfront about it. Confirm your more constructive and sturdy footing, and free them from any tentativeness they maintain around you both.

In business settings, it's often imperative that others are advised of the details of your agreement. It will likely change how the pair of you interact with colleagues, or operate processes that affect a company. Sometimes an agreed message – a **communiqué** – is prepared for those impacted – a statement in a meeting (preferred), email, memo, briefing note.

Such statements should be pre-cleared now, before you conclude this conversation. Ask and answer, "Who needs to know about this?"

And... breathe

With these finalities completed, take a well-earned moment to reflect upon what's happened. Let the impact sink in. Set your paper aside, sit back and look your VIP in the eye. Express your gratitude to them for sticking with you throughout this conversation. Appreciate what you created together in the past, and the positive difference this resolution agreement will make in your future

Let them know you look forward to being close again, and imagine the possibilities that may arise as a result. Let the optimism flow!

> "Leonora, I'm so proud that we have had this talk and worked through this issue. We are a better team now.
>
> I was jumping the gun when I got upset and that launched a series of events I wish I could reel back.

> Your willingness to take part in this process and put yourself out there to improve how we work together cements your place as a leader and key contributor here.

We need to set a date to bring our teams together. Thank you."

"It's been an honor, Dave. I am lucky to have a colleague who is prepared to work this hard to get past a problem.

Oh, and by the way, we rethought your invitation and with this done, Ray and I are coming to the big birthday bash."

In the end; arrival, safe and sound

Congratulations. You have a right to be proud! Who wouldn't be? This process is not for those who seek the easy way. Coming to grips with issues that are loaded with controversy and self-protection is very hard work.

The Resolution Protocol is a complete pathway, and a voyage that has brought you to the wonderful destination you had hoped for.

Just as with *kintsugi*, your restored bucket is now a vessel ready to receive new injections of mutual experience, to hold the trust and all the confident expectation that you will grow and prosper together. You can laugh in knowing awareness, rejoice at the gold of your exquisite joint effort reflecting in sunlight of the new morning, all the more startling for having emerged from shadows.

FIXING FRACTURES

Epilogue

The occasion was Ron's 70th birthday. The expansive venue was all decked out, and 70 guests were seated at white-clothed tables, looking out over the 18th green. Many a great golf game had ended there, on the undulating contours of that surface.

The afternoon wasn't devoted to sport but to celebration. Cut to the speeches and presentations... they befitted Ron, the successful and much-admired head of an influential company like Dugmore.

As the toasts proceeded, David and Leonora stood in the wings. A gift-wrapped package was propped between them as they awaited their cue from Alfredo, Ron's friend, and the event MC.

When the time came, they moved forward in lockstep each holding one end of a slender box with a cube appended at one end. Reaching the head table, David spoke first:

> "Ron, you've had such a great impact on me, Leonora, and so many others. I'll never forget that day you gave me a game-breaker chance to join your great company."

Leonora chimed in,

> "I kind of came in the back door at Dugmore, but I'll echo David... I feel very lucky to be here, and to have made such a career out of this work. Who knew that would happen!? Well, Ron did, I guess...

Dave and I thought we'd go together to get you a little memento to celebrate today – something you apparently wouldn't get for yourself."

She and David leaned forward, handing Ron the gift.

Now Ron, for all his position, was a bit of a cheapskate when it came to spending money on himself. But the two had done a bit of digging, and learned from the club pro that Ron had been endlessly muttering about a certain aspect of his game.

He tore at the wrapping like a kid.

"You didn't… It's the newest Scotty Cameron! Well, isn't that a treat! Thanks so much, you two!"

He knew that his putting tensions would ease with this fancy putter.

Then he gave them a private, knowing wink.

"And I know what it took for the two of you to do this together. It will make this great putter that much more special to me. I'll think about you both every time I take it out of my bag."

David and Leonora shared a look, and chuckled a bit as they moved back to their seats.

Afterword and recap

Publishing this handbook has been my goal for a while. I felt compelled. Anyone, anywhere should have access to the Resolution Protocol, the Relationship Mindset, and these supporting materials. John Konstanturos was my mentor, and tutored me in this approach back in the 1990s. Since then, I expanded upon it extensively in my practice. As far as I know, I'm the only person he trained in this full approach. I cannot let this knowledge end with me.

Here's a recap of the process this book has traversed, through a different lens.

The purpose of a resolution conversation is to repair a fracture that holds two parties apart.

- It is to effect a reconciliation and significantly adjust an essential, but 'stuck' connection in your life.
- The character of the conversation is a wholehearted exploration of the foundations of a relationship between two people. As they talk, they remain competent, in possession of themselves, and unreserved in their pursuit of truth and healing together.
- It is not to dispense with a troubling individual or to deliver the final telling blow in a dispute.
- It is not to equip oneself with new and superior weapons, for what John Konstanturos called, 'more enlightened blaming'.

The role of the initiator of this corrective conversation is to:

- Hit the nerve – face an unsettling situation directly and deal with it, even though emotions are aroused.
- Get right to the source – the core of past failures.
- Keep the other person wholly engaged – ensure they follow along with what is said, as the conversation tackles a highly-charged dispute.
- Stay with it all the way to a comprehensive and satisfying conclusion, so that both get to a much better place.

The driving mechanisms of this approach are the Resolution Protocol, coupled with the Relationship Mindset. Together they help the initiator lead the conversation through the Flow of the distinct sections, armed with the Pre-work:

- Being extremely specific about one single incident – not a barrage of similar cases
- Detailing the facts of the incident, just as by giving evidence in a courtroom; no hearsay, just what the initiator saw, heard, read, or produced personally
- Relating the emotions this incident raised in the initiator – mad, sad, glad, scared – and discovering the impacts on identity
- Having the initiator take radical ownership for their part in the creating or sustaining the fracture
- Asking the other party to detail their version
- Getting the other party to disclose the impact of the incident on them
- Stating how the initiator expects, at minimum, to reframe/reorient the relationship going forward
- Entering a full and mutual dialogue, working together to shape a better basis for getting along

- Restating a new understanding and affirming their new bond

Great care is taken throughout, so that the respondent can track what's unfolding and be a full and willing collaborator in creating a superb outcome.

Ten years from now, both participants will be able to speak of their successful resolution conversation as *a turnaround moment.*

And finally, here are **the strengths of this approach to resolution**:

1. **It is orderly**
   Most dysfunctional fights between people are free-for-alls. This is the main reason they never end, and why they only result in an ever-widening gap between the participants.

2. **It is set up to neutralize power**
   Power has importance, but true leaders don't get things done by crushing others. They prefer to enroll and enlist them as co-venturers.

3. **It is civil**
   It allows people to keep their heads together while dealing with an emotionally difficult situation. Dignity is retained and reinforced.

4. **It is developmental**
   You cannot help but grow, and expand your capabilities by learning this approach and putting it into practice.

5. **It is optimistic**

It brings hope back into the equation.

It works.

It just works.

Appendices

Appendix A – It won't work when...

The Resolution Protocol isn't a cure-all! This approach to finally settling nagging and important relationship problems is potent and clean. But circumstances do exist where it cannot overcome the challenges. I've outlined some below, as they constitute limitations to what can and should be attempted with this process.

This information is given not to fuel excuses and rationalizations as to why resolution should not be tried. In my practice I have many times been confronted with, "Nothing can be done!" Then followed that with an intense exchange that adjusted relationships onto a substantially new footing.

Arming doubters is not the purpose here. However, there are limits. Being aware of them is essential.

Where won't the Protocol work?

When people are completely closed off to, or incapable of changing themselves or their approach

I recently came upon a situation in which the patriarch of a family company unilaterally reduced the compensation of his daughter – the President. She was livid and totally demotivated, since there was no agreed basis for this action. She shouldered all the work to run the franchise, while her brother lolled about. Dad practiced classic *seagull management* – dropping by the office from time to time to jigger with matters, then leave. He also carefully guarded his role as keeper of the numbers, and stonewalled any efforts to change things. And, he was also beginning to show signs of memory loss.

Some people become increasingly resistant to learning. They are no longer open to hearing what others have to say, to receiving feedback or suggestions for change. Their life of growth and meaningful personal interaction is waning. It's too bad. They are unable to endure or learn from encounters in a world that sometimes doesn't function as they desire. They enjoy only self-affirming interactions. The Protocol cannot overcome this basic closing-off.

The same logic also excludes people who labor under psychological conditions that prevent give-and-take in a true conversation. They may be personality disordered – paranoid, have acute anger issues, or otherwise be mentally incapable of substantive interaction.

I always preceded my consulting resolution work with an engagement conference to assess such dimensions. It's critical to determine whether the players can look each other in the eye, can engage capably under a regime of rules and procedures, and can agree to work together toward achieving resolution.

When you consider using this material on your own, you won't be able to insist on such preconditions. Size the situation up for yourself but err on the side that this Protocol probably *can* work.

When there are structural impossibilities

Sometimes, there is no prospect for the Protocol because of distance – in power, location, or role – which prevents the close, face-to-face meeting(s) that this process demands. Those factors are so constraining as to make this work near impossible.

One person may simply be too insignificant to another to justify devoting any time to the issue. This is true in situations where there are large gaps in hierarchy between individuals, or where the power differential is too large to bridge.

On the other hand, when true, strong leaders discover they have caused heartburn with a lower-ranked employee, they are often so growth oriented they will want to rectify the situation and learn from the encounter.

Or, even if family members are located far away, they may be so concerned, they want to meet. They just can't stand the idea that a barrier exists between themselves and their relative.

It's just reality that reaching resolution requires both willingness and face-to-face time, however those may be arranged. Minor differences might be worked through remotely, but significant ones? Being unable to see physical reactions during the conversation is a very big reason why I think the distance issue is a barrier.

In this era of increasing intense and intimate video conferencing experiences between people, we have generally become more comfortable with this type of interaction. I still believe however that video technology is a poor substitute for observable reality. In our pandemic exposed world, people may have no option but to meet remotely; video interactions may be the only choice. In this case, you'll have to be much more attentive to subtle reactions and responses. A very real to desire to attempt resolution can overcome the hurdles.

Due to overwhelming market, financial or personal realities

In the business world, there are occasions when there just isn't time available to devote to serious interpersonal work. A market collapse, a major executive defection, a merger, a downturn that affects business viability – these are events that take priority over the interpersonal. Ongoing discord adds friction to the actions needed to deal with such situations, but the parties just have to manage through it.

Similarly in families, if someone is faced with a financial emergency, suffering an acute health crisis, or dealing with a tragedy or death, it's not time to pile on an interpersonal difference. They're already overstretched and cannot engage to the extent resolution requires.

When people can't even agree on a means to address difference

Every transition must start somewhere. Sometimes people are so lost in their opposition to another that they can't even acknowledge or respond to an overture to work on the situation.

Say an individual suggests this resolution work to their counterpart. But that party cannot stomach a working intervention, even in the face of a mountain of dysfunction and downstream cost. They can only find fault with the initiator's suggestions:

That'll never work! – when a method is proposed

You want me to do WHAT? – when logistics and convenience are used to mask unwillingness

Get out of my sight!

If this is going to work, you must somehow reach a launch point. The other party will at least have to allow an initial venture into the sore spots.

Here are some softer strategies you might try to bring an inflexible counterparty to the table:

- Write a letter – when the recipient has a written proposal in hand, they can mull it over and think about the offer in ways a verbal request won't convey.
- Make a direct appeal to the heart – allow your bruised spirit to come to the forefront, and speak to the intensity of your need to resolve what happened between you. Plead for the chance to change things.
- Use a trusted intermediary – sometimes there is a friend, counsellor or other caring individual who will agree to broach the possibility of resolution to one or both parties.

None of this means you shouldn't try. If the other party completely shuts you down, then the last alternative is to adjust to living your life without the benefit of this relationship in its fullest form.

Whatever the limits, fortune favors the bold. Go for it. The possibility of freedom from ongoing grief is too compelling to ignore.

Appendix B – Recommended reading

- **Fierce Conversations** – Achieving Success at Work & in Life, One Conversation at a Time
  Susan Scott

- **Difficult Conversations** – How to Discuss What Matters Most
  Stone, Patton, & Heen

- **When the Body Says No** – The Cost of Hidden Stress
  Gabor Maté

- **The Communication Catalyst** – The Fast (but not stupid) Track to Value for Customers, Investors and Employees
  Connolly & Rianoshek

Fixing Fractures Toolkit

Download printable versions at *DougBouey.com/ffdownloads*

The Resolution Protocol on a Page

The Protocol is effective because of its stepwise separation of topics. It is a simple, clean recipe to follow in a resolution conversation, that maximizes potential for correction and change.

STEP 1	Describe **your role and relationship** to the other person.
STEP 2	Outline the **facts of a single incident** that led to the relationship break.
STEP 3	Express ***your* emotional reaction** to the situation and its impact on your identity.
STEP 4	**Declare your part** in creating or continuing the situation.
STEP 5	**Listen to *their* version** of what happened, and *their* emotional reaction.
STEP 6	Describe **your expectations** of what is required to set matters right.
STEP 7	**Negotiate** a path forward to rectify the situation.
STEP 8	**Clarify** your new agreement, and **affirm** your restored **common purpose**.

The Resolution Guidance System on a Page

Anger Aggression	Care and Compassion	Fear Avoidance
• Erupting	• **Balanced**	• Making nice
• Yelling	• **Optimal**	• Avoiding
• Sarcasm	• **Anchored**	• Sloughing off
• Arguing	• **Opening**	• Minimizing
• Lashing out	• **Sensing**	• Manipulating
• Glowering	**surroundings**	• Going blank
• Manipulating	• **Taking deep**	• Shying away
• Overwhelming	**body breaths**	• Indifference
• Overcoming	• **Relaxed**	• Silence
• Bullying	• **Empathetic**	• Impassivity
• Attacking		• Crying
• Breathing sharply inward		• Emoting
• Tunnel vision		• Dramatizing
• Freezing [to restrain aggression]		• Smoothing over
		• Shallow breathing
		• Scanning for escapes
		• Freezing [to not make it worse]

The Preparation Worksheet

The Incident

Describe the one situation that serves as the focal point.

Step 1 - Roles and Relationship

- **Roles** *Name the frameworks that bring you two together (e.g., supervisor, partner, team member).*
- **Role characteristics** *Describe the dynamics of how it works when you are each performing optimally in your role.*
- **Relationship** *Set out the ways you relate to each other (e.g., friend, aunt, sports coach).*
- **Relationship characteristics** *Describe the dynamics of what your relationship looks like when it's going great.*

Step 2 - The Facts

Use a timeline to capture all elements of what occurred from the start of the incident to its conclusion.

Start   Events   End

Evidence for each timeline element

Event	Evidence – *only what you saw, heard, said, produced*

Step 3 - The Feelings

- *Describe the emotions you experienced as a result of the incident (e.g., mad / sad / glad / scared).*
- **Identity impact** *Describe aspects of your own sense of identity that have been damaged, and how this incident reflects on who you believe yourself to be.*

 "...and those are mine to deal with"

Step 4 - 100%→0% Accountability

- *Review Step 1 roles for clarity*
- *Detail all the ways you created or continued the incident.*

I woulda...

I coulda...

I shoulda...

Step 5 - VIP's view

Listen to their version of the incident, their facts, their feelings. Ready some open-ended questions to encourage them to reveal more details. Avoid questions that start with 'why'.

Step 6 - Intended outcome

*Set out characteristics of the new arrangement that **you** want to include as part of a restored or renovated role or relationship.*

 Use open, non-restrictive terminology. Refer to your preparation for Step 1, but be ready to adapt as your awareness expands.

Step 7 - Negotiation

- **List solution options/ideas** *Write down whatever is surfaced or proposed.*
- **Short list** *Identify the scenarios selected for further development.*
- **The details** Build out the scenarios to enhance their realism and workability, and include implementation aspects.

(!)   *"What might sabotage this solution?"*

- **Magic Five** Which elements are to be introduced and/or included in the proposed solution.
- **Rinse and repeat** List other incidents revealed when you asked, 'What might sabotage this solution?' Use a separate sheet of paper for each incident, and capture their details, as necessary, e.g.:

1.	*Roles*	5.	*VIP's version*
2.	*The facts*	6.	*Outcome*
3.	*The reactions*		*statement*
4.	*100%→0%*	7.	*Negotiation*
	accountability	8.	*Confirmation*

Step 8 - Confirmation and commitment

- *Restate your agreed resolution proposal.*
- **Common purpose** *Outline aspects of your best relationship that emerged as a result of reaching resolution, to reiterate to each other.*
- **Communiqué** *List items you need to share with others about the outcome of this talk.*

Fixing Fractures – the fast lane

A handbook

- The Resolution Protocol is an approach to settling serious, daunting problems between people.
- Can it work in all situations? There are limiting conditions (Appendix A), but it is suitable for bringing most fractured relationships to closure.

The travelers and the journey

- Discipline and commitment to the full process are required to achieve resolution. There are:
  o Concepts to learn and preparations to carry out
  o Snags and sensitivities to navigate
- You need courage to stay the course, face the issue, the other person, and yourself. You are likely to step up to the challenge because you feel you must, and because you care about the other party – your Very Important Person (VIP).
- Taking a tough situation over the finish line to resolution is one of the most satisfying things you will ever do in your life.

When is it time?

- Assess the need for this conversation by examining how you persistently think and feel about the relationship:
  - Trust between you and your VIP has been broken. You feel betrayed.
  - You think about the situation over and over; it occupies your mind incessantly.
  - You regret the incident.
  - You dread any forthcoming encounters.
  - You feel compelled by your conscience to act and restore the broken relationship.

Get organized for the trip

- Four components are required for a resolution conversation:
  - **The Resolution Protocol** – the eight process steps; the *program*
  - **The Relationship Mindset** – the perspective that orients you to success; the *operating system*
  - **The Pre-Work** – indispensable advance work; the Preparation Worksheet
  - **The Flow** – exercising leadership so the talk is orderly and disciplined
- These elements, working together, allow two competent people to address a highly-charged and difficult subject, remaining whole and self-possessed throughout.
- Adhering to the structure of the resolution conversation is as important as what is said during the actual talk.

The road you travel; one incident

- Choose one incident from the many that have contributed to your difficult situation. Any one will do; it focuses your preparation and keeps the talk clean, crisp, and clear.
- Your aim is to address what's gone wrong, rather than win the dispute.

Set the date; start the car

- Advance preparation lets you confidently take on a conversation that will likely be turbulent, but will work.
- Your completed Preparation Worksheet clarifies your thinking, helps you stay focused and able to handle any conversation detours.
- Complete the worksheet for Protocol Steps 1, 2, 3, 4 and 6, following guidance in the appropriate chapters.
- Worksheet in hand, raise the issue with your VIP, and set a date and time for the conversation. But be ready to start the discussion immediately if necessary.
- Trust that your intentions, the integrity of your approach and this structured process will help you through the introduction of the topic.

Step 1 - Buckle in; my roles and relationship to you

- List all the roles and ways you link to each other, including ties you have at work, as friends, at home, out in the world. Add some details – purpose, scope, character of each.

- Looking back at the bonds you had when they were strong will help you be clear on the outcome of this conversation – a new, improved, optimal version of your relationship.
- Shape what you've written into a conversation opener. Imagine your VIP nodding along as you speak.

Step 2 - The facts; your bumpy road

- No two people see a situation the same way.
- Outline the details of your selected single incident on the Preparation Worksheet
  - o Lay it out on a timeline and describe the supporting evidence for each event.
- Stick to facts only; anything else will prevent you from moving forward together.
  - o Facts are: what you said, what they said to you, what you both heard together, or what can be produced.

Rest stop! A guidance system for a turbulent ride

- The Relationship Guidance System (RGS) is the essential guiding instrument you use to navigate and interpret emotions that arise during the talk.
- The RGS helps you visualize and confirm what your senses and intuition tell you. It operates like a vehicle GPS and safety alert system combined. It helps you spot when your chat has strayed off course, and recover.

- You use the RGS to neutralize diverting reactions from your VIP or yourself.
- To keep the conversation from veering left or right on the RGS Gauge (and off track from your goal), keep centered on your purpose. Counteract diversions with words expressed from your heart.
- Refer to the *RGS on a Page* (in the Appendix) to name a reaction, understand its source, and respond appropriately.
- Body sensibility gives you early clues when your talk crosses your VIP's boundaries.

Step 3 - The driver; emotions and identity

- Often you are in this mess because of feelings, but they are not the whole story.
- The Protocol's structure puts emotions in their place – just one of many elements that must be discussed.
- Your feelings must be fully disclosed, as information to be understood. Beyond emotions, the deeper impacts to your *identity* must also be exposed.
- You own your feelings. *'These feelings are mine to deal with'* is a consistent and critical phrase you use in Step 3.
- Use the RGS to stay steady throughout your disclosure of emotion.
- Warning – 'feelings' can frequently be used to manipulate (*you made me ...*).

Step 4 – Over the bridge; take radical ownership

- Step 4 unlocks the door to resolution. It demands that you take radical ownership for what went wrong.
- You take 100% responsibility and leave 0% responsibility to the other. You caused it. Totally.
- You take accountability not to put yourself down, but to get straight to the heart of the issue, and claim your willingness to do what it takes to fix it things.
- It's not a phony stance. You don't absorb responsibility for all the other person's actions. You stay within your proper role in this relationship.
- Your ego will hate this; it wants to keep you in the right. But by protecting you, it keeps you in a poor place. With 20/20 hindsight, put your ego aside and see just how you fell short of a high standard.
- Look back at your Step 1 and 2 preparation – review the optimal roles, and traverse the timeline of events.
- *Woulda / Shoulda / Coulda* are key guides to help you identify your shortcomings.

Pit stop! Amp up awareness; be ready to really listen

- Maintaining acute awareness of your counterpart is as important as what you each say.
- Active Listening and Body Sensibility are two techniques that help you be attentive, and to quiet and focus your mind.
- Unexpected reactions will occur during your talk. If you focus on listening and observation, you will

be less self-absorbed, and more able to use the RGS to adapt to whatever occurs.

- Differences between people are natural and a part of life; they are not bad or wrong.
- The relational skills you practice here will serve you well in all areas of your life.

Step 5 - The view from *there*

- Stop talking now, and listen. Your sole role is to draw the other person out, to let them tell their version.
- You may feel nervous about giving over control of the conversation. It will be okay. You still guide the Flow.
- Expect them to react. Expect to feel a lot. Tame your urge to argue or push back.
- Let the conversation unfold as it must; stay grounded in the Relationship Mindset.
- Practise the skills you learned last chapter; use the RGS to stay balanced, and track toward your destination.
- Ask as many open-ended questions as you need to get at all the details.

Step 6 - Recenter on your destination; *recalculating...*

- Take the lead in the conversation again, to aim it back to your original objective – the restoration and enhancement of your roles and relationship.
- You prepare a statement of your objectives ahead of time;

o   Look to how you described your optimal roles and relationship in Step 1 preparation. Check the ideals you compared yourself to in Step 4.

- Be ready to alter your objectives after hearing your VIP's version of the incident.

- Maintain the Relationship Mindset and use the RGS to help you choose your words.

- The details you disclose now about what you want to achieve are the template for what you get at the end of this process.

Step 7 - Negotiation; onward with your adventure

- Together with your VIP, negotiate a proposal to resolve the situation. Brainstorm ideas, prioritize them, then expand on the most suitable combination of solution options.

- Intermix *Magic Five* statements to address the deeper, spiritual damage caused by the break, and to restore trust.

- Test and fortify your proposed solutions against failure by asking, '*What might sabotage this solution?*'

- Other past incidents/situations will surface. Process each one with your VIP, using the same approach that brought you this far. Use the caring, collaborative environment you have built to persevere.

- True resolution is at hand.

Step 8 - Arrive in style; confirmation and commitment

- Document the components of your agreed outcome – the adjustments, *Magic Five* elements, and any other arrangements you've agreed to.
  - o Address any omissions or glitches you encounter as you recap.
- Verbally affirm your new, more wholesome basis of association going forward.
- Let others who've been affected by your low trust know what has changed between you, so they can adapt and act.
- Stand back and let the joy of the work sink in...

Acknowledgements

Above all the substance of this book is thanks to John Konstanturos. John was an innovator whose euphemistically entitled *team building workshops* drove top groups to realignments that many thought were beyond reach. John's approach was simple. People want to work together productively. Incidents occur that pull them away from that natural orientation. If not resolved, those showstoppers divide them and divert them from their common purpose. So, if what has divided them can be repaired, they will come together and get back to pursuing their intended goal. When teaching the Resolution Protocol and the Relationship Mindset to these groups, he brought pairs together to the front of the room and put the question blocking their trust in each other on the line. They worked it through. With the barrier removed, they united. Simple. Direct.

We who benefit from this approach now are in his debt. John's widow, Jackie Townsend Konstanturos has been a booster of this book all along. She sees it as the book John didn't write. Ozzie Gontang, legendary Vistage Chair from San Diego, was instrumental in clearing the path to her endorsement.

Susan Scott's belief in this book and contribution of a forward was a turning point to delivering this handbook.

Books cannot be concise without outside eyes seeing through early versions to the essence of the message and bringing it forward. I was very fortunate in having those critical views lent to me by Peter Buchanan, Michael Dargie, Walt Sutton, Susan Miller, Joyce Hookings, Ken Juba, Scott Morris, and others. They helped boil down the content to what you see. My son Evan introduced me to the art of *kintsugi* after reading the drafts, and I am grateful for his support and that compelling metaphor, so apt for this book's subject matter. But it was my brother-in-law Wayne Biggs who sat with me of a summer afternoon on his patio and carved back my first manuscript from what was then 280+ pages, down to the true handbook you have here.

Before and after that came the real work of shaping the expression for maximum clarity and truth to intent. The dialogue with my gifted and patient editor, Lois Wozney, was absolutely the key to concision in the material result. She is a gem and I treasure her follow up and drive. The delightful, artful additions of my able friend Alejandro Anaya from San Miguel de Allende added just the right touch of levity and character to the text. And the later contributions of Michael Dargie helped bring public attention to the book.

My indulgent partner Elaine let the whole process flow and encouraged me to finish.

To all, my limitless gratitude.

Douglas Robert Bouey
DougBouey.com
FixingFractures.com

Profiles

John Konstanturos
Founder, CEO, Continuous Renewal

John's career as a consultant and trainer originated during the riots and chaos of the '60s. As a young supervisor in the Los Angeles Police Department, he was involved in putting down riots in the streets of Los Angeles. Called upon to find more effective and peaceful ways of preventing wild and emotional demonstrations from becoming riots, John's task  force developed several innovative and highly effective procedures, management systems and strategies. These were later adopted as the model plan by the International Association of Chiefs of Police, and are still widely used today.

The communication, management and people skills John learned during his 26-year career with the LAPD laid the foundation for his later success as a business consultant. Although he held a Master's Degree in Management from Pepperdine University, John attributed the unique character of his success to his own personal, emotional, and spiritual development. He believed that personal and organizational renewal generates whole, well-balanced leaders and more open, trusting relationships – qualities that are especially needed in today's demanding leadership circles. Helping individuals and organizations develop the skills to sustain their own process of renewal represented the essence of his work.

A Commitment to Personal Renewal

Upon leaving the LAPD in 1982, John launched his career as an independent consultant. For more than 25 years, he helped business leaders and their organizations create transformational change and achieve higher levels of performance. Using an innovative process that combined ancient wisdom with leading-edge developmental techniques, John coached CEOs and senior executives to improve their leadership skills, build high-performing teams, and create cultures that embraced personal accountability as a core value and essential creator of success.

John's work took him around the world and included prominent clients such as:

- The Attorney General of the U. S.
- The Governor of Florida
- MGM Grand Companies
- 1st National Bank
- Eli Lilly/AME
- Sylvania
- Heinz
- Bumblebee Seafoods
- YPO
- Seiko Instruments
- New York, New York Hotel & Casino
- U. S. Army
- American Hospital Association

John worked for 10 years as a group Chairman for Vistage International (formerly The Executive Committee, or TEC), where he coached and mentored more than two dozen CEOs each month, helping them to identify opportunities, resolve problems and position their companies for long-term growth and profitability. It was during this period that John learned the importance of ongoing personal renewal by the leader at the top, and the commitment at all levels to organizational renewal.

John spoke about team building to 450 TEC groups throughout the world and was awarded Speaker of the Year in 2010.

John lived in Del Mar, CA with his second wife Jackie until his passing in 2019.

Douglas Bouey

Doug is a mentor to many presidents and executives, and a leader of growth processes for mid-market businesses.

He was a pioneer Chair for The Executive Committee [TEC in Canada, Vistage in the US]. His group launched in 1986 and he continued to Chair his peer gathering of presidents for 32 years. He was presented the *Cope Award* in 2009, as most outstanding Chair (worldwide).

His work is focused on connection:

- of leaders to their learning and expansion
- of businesses to their market
- of people to purpose
- of team members to each other and work under the umbrella of companies.

Douglas met John Konstanturos in 1985 while starting his TEC group. Their fascinating bond grew into a long and deep friendship. John and Doug collaborated on the first gathering of 10+ year TEC Chairs at Borrego Springs, CA that evolved into the *Keepers of the Flame* annual conference in Boulder, CO.

John presented this revolutionary approach to resolution to Doug's TEC group at a retreat in Emerald Lake, British Columbia; Douglas was hooked. He went on to learn the methodology and to put it into practice while John mentored him.

Doug's consulting practice included and embraced John's *'Team Building'* workshops from that point forward. The material was adapted over time as Doug's extensive training in psychotherapy and business planning was infused into the core concepts.

Doug conducted *Relationship Rehab* for many mid-market companies over the years. Once or twice in each year he would field a call for work to fashion 'impossible' reconciliations between warring principals in a company. After careful engagement, he would deploy the Resolution Protocol to get to the bottom of fractured executive and ownership groups. Douglas made a team out of them to the surprise and delight of the participants and those relying on them.

In his mentoring work, Douglas taught his clients the methodology for their own, self-led rectifications of broken alliances.

Douglas continues to develop and publish written works:

- Jaunts: Mexico – Doug's adventures in lesser-visited places in Mexico
- Let go of the Rope – on adult later-life transitions (2022)
- The Warrior Strategy, and The Five Dimensions of Vision – companion volumes to this book

He lives on Hornby Island in British Columbia, Canada, and in San Miguel de Allende, Mexico, while remaining based in Calgary, Alberta, Canada. He paints, writes, and walks in company with his spouse Elaine. He has two grown children, Jane and Evan, of whom he is very proud.

DougBouey.com

Cutting up an Ox

Chuang-Tzu (c 369 – c 286 B.C E.)

Prince Wen Hui's cook
Was cutting up an ox.
Out went a hand,
Down went a shoulder,
He planted a foot,
He pressed with a knee,
The ox fell apart
With a whisper,
The bright cleaver murmured
Like a gentle wind.
Rhythm! Timing!
Like a sacred dance,
Like "The Mulberry Grove,"
Like ancient harmonies!
"Good work!" the prince exclaimed,
"Your method is faultless!"
"Method?" said the cook
Laying aside his cleaver,
"What I follow is Tao
Beyond all methods!
"When I first began
To cut up oxen
I would see before me
The whole ox
All in one mass.
"After three years
I no longer saw this mass.
I saw the distinctions.
"But now, I see nothing
With the eye. My whole being
Apprehends.
My senses are idle. The spirit
Free to work without plan
Follows its own instinct
Guided by natural line,

By the secret opening, the hidden space,
My cleaver finds its own way.
I cut through no joint, chop no bone.
"A good cook needs a new chopper
Once a year – he cuts.
A poor cook needs a new one
Every month – he hacks!
"I have used this same cleaver
Nineteen years.
It has cut up
A thousand oxen.
Its edge is as keen
As if newly sharpened.
"There are spaces in the joints;
The blade is thin and keen:
When this thinness
Finds that space
There is all the room you need!
It goes like a breeze!
Hence, I have this cleaver nineteen years
As if newly sharpened!
"True, there are sometimes
Tough joints. I feel them coming,
I slow down, I watch closely,
Hold back, barely move the blade,
And whump! The part falls away
Landing like a clod of earth.
"Then I withdraw the blade,
I stand still
And let the joy of the work
Sink in.
I clean the blade
And put it away."
Prince Wen Hui said,
"This is it! My cook has shown me
How I ought to live
My own life!"

Lois Wozney

Lois is a 'semi-retired' business consultant with a breadth and depth of experience earned in the trenches of corporate Canada. A born communicator, her career grew consistently alongside her ability to engage and encourage people to improve and change.

A decently skilled writer and dogged technology wrangler, she has lately embarked on a grand egression from her *as-built* career to the *on-spec* path ahead ... one that's chock-full of shiny, fascinating things. Birthing books with Doug Bouey (bookwifery?) is just one of these.

Lois is an avid reader with special interest in history and culture, and enjoys travel, bold red wines, and urban gardening. She lives in Calgary, Alberta, Canada with her abiding husband of long standing, three entitled cats, and two-plus-one fine adult children who only mock her occasionally, with much love.

Alejandro Anaya

Born in Torreon, Mexico, Alejandro Anaya has always been passionate about art, cinema, and telling stories through drawing, painting, engraving, and writing.

His quest to constantly evolve his visual discourse has led him to experiment with various mixed media techniques, with which he seeks to reflect his fascination for human expression and the diversity of views on the world.

Above all, Alejandro focuses on creating characters freely, and through spontaneous strokes, in order to express the imperfection and genius of the human imagination.

Today he lives happily in San Miguel de Allende, working as an artist, writer, and creative director, dedicating most of his time to art and cultural promotion.

Instagram: @alejandroanayavisualartist

Facebook: Alejandro Anaya Art

Manufactured by Amazon.ca
Bolton, ON

24639933R00127